THE CONTRIBUTION OF THE JUBBULPORE MUTINY TO INDIA'S FREEDOM

Did the INA also have a Role?

THE CONTRIBUTION OF THE JUBBULPORE MUTINY TO INDIA'S FREEDOM

Did the INA also have a Role?

Maj Gen VK Singh

KW Publishers Pvt Ltd
New Delhi

Copyright © 2022 Maj Gen VK Singh

All rights reserved. No part of this publication may be reproduced, stored in a retrieval system, or transmitted in any form or by any means, electronic, mechanical, photocopying, recording or otherwise, without the prior written permission of the copyright owner.

ISBN   978-93-94915-08-4   Paperback
ISBN   978-93-94915-09-1   ebook

Published in India by Kalpana Shukla

KW Publishers Pvt Ltd
4676/21, First Floor, Ansari Road
Daryaganj, New Delhi 110002
Phone: +91 11 43528107
Marketing: kw@kwpub.in
Editorial: production@kwpub.in
Website: www.kwpub.in

The content of this book is the sole expression and opinion of its authors, and not of the publishers. The publishers in no manner is liable for any opinion or views expressed by the author. While best efforts have been made in preparing the book, the publishers makes no representations or warranties of any kind and assumes no liabilities of any kind with respect to the accuracy or completeness of the content and specifically disclaims any implied warranties of merchantability or fitness of use of a particular purpose.

The publisher believes that the contents of this book do not violate any existing copyright/intellectual property of others in any manner whatsoever. However, in case any source has not been duly attributed, the publisher may be notified in writing for necessary action.

Contents

Abbreviations	vii
1. Introduction	1
2. The Naval Mutiny—1946	14
3. The Air Force Mutiny—1946	40
4. Brief History of The Corps of Signals	55
5. The Army (Signals) Mutiny at Jubbulpore—1946	79
6. The Indian National Army—A Brief History	102
7. Subhas Bose & The INA—Some Unanswered Questions	122
8. Nationalism in The Indian Army	143
9. Did The Army Signals Mutiny at Jubbulore Play A Part in India's Independence?	159
Bibliography	182

Abbreviations

ADC	Aide de Camp
AG	Adjutant General
AOC	Army Ordnance Corps, Air Officer Commanding
AOC-in-C	Air Officer Commanding-in-Chief
BBC	British Broadcasting Corporation
BM	Brigade Major
BOAC	British Overseas Airways Corporation
BOR	British Other Rank(s)
CCO	Central Communications Office
CGS	Chief of General Staff
C-in-C	Commander-in-Chief
CID	Criminal Investigation Department
CIH	Central India Horse
CO	Commanding Officer
COS	Chief of Staff
COSC	Chiefs of Staff Committee
DFC	Distinguished Flying Cross
DMI	Director of Military Intelligence
DMO	Director of Military Operations
DSO	Distinguished Service Order
ECO	Emergency Commissioned Officer
FOCRIN	Flag Officer Commanding Royal Indian Navy
GHQ	General Headquarters
GOC	General Officer Commanding
GOC-in-C	General Officer Commanding-in-Chief
GS	General Staff
HQ	Headquarters

IAF	Indian Air Force
IAFVR	Indian Air Force Volunteer Reserve
ICO	Indian Commissioned Officer
ICS	Indian Civil Service
IMA	Indian Military Academy
INA	Indian National Army
IOM	Indian Order of Merit
IOR	Indian Other Rank(s)
IPS	Indian Police Service
JCO	Junior Commissioned Officer
KCIO	King's Commissioned Indian Officer
MC	Military Cross
MLI	Mahratta (now Maratha) Light Infantry
MI	Military Intelligence
MO	Military Operations
MT	Mechanical Transport
NCO	Non Commissioned Officer
NWFP	North-West Frontier Province
OR	Other Rank(s)
PBF	Punjab Boundary Force
POW	Prisoner of War
QMG	Quarter Master General
RAF	Royal Air Force
RIAF	Royal Indian Air Force
RIASC	Royal Indian Service Corps
2/Lt	Second Lieutenant
STC	Signal Training Centre
VC	Victoria Cross
VCO	Viceroy's Commissioned Officer
WRIN	Women's Royal Indian Navy

1
Introduction

The Indian Armed Forces played an important part in the grant of independence to India in 1947. Among the three services, the most significant role was that of the Indian Army, particularly the Indian Signal Corps, now known as the Corps of Signals. The role of the Indian Armed Forces in the struggle for freedom from British rule has not been properly documented or publicised. The general public remains unaware and the nation's leaders have never acknowledged or appreciated the part played by the military in this important chapter of our history. As a result, the affected personnel have not been given recognition or reward for their efforts. In some cases, they were deprived of their livelihood and liberty, without compensation. There is a need to undo this injustice and acquaint the nation with Armed Forces' contribution to the freedom movement.

India's independence from British rule in 1947 was achieved after a protracted and sustained struggle that lasted several decades. It has a unique place in World History since it was characterised by non-violence, a novel form of rebellion popularised by Mahatma Gandhi. It was the only instance when a colonial power not only relinquished authority voluntarily but also advanced the date of its departure. Though essentially non-violent, the movement had elements that involved the use of force, the most notable being the Indian National Army led by Subhas Chandra Bose, who attained iconic status after his death. Ironically, the INA was created with the help of Japan, a country with which India, then under British rule, was at war. During World War II, few Indians had heard of the INA, which did not have the backing of the National Congress, the party that was leading the struggle for freedom.

However, after the war ended, fortuitous events such as the Red Fort trials made the country aware of the INA. Overnight, members of the INA, who had until then been regarded as turncoats by their colleagues in the Indian Army, became heroes.

The saga of the INA has been well documented by scores of Indian and foreign historians. A large number of accounts has been written by members of the INA, extolling their role in the freedom struggle. Several Indian and foreign historians have written books on the subject, relying on personal accounts of INA veterans and official records of the governments of India and Japan. There are scores of biographies of Bose, but, except for a few, most are hagiographies. The lay reader will find enough to sustain his interest, but the meticulous researcher is often disappointed. The anomalies and disparities in the different narratives are too glaring to be overlooked, and one sometimes wonders whether he is reading fact or fiction. At the end of it, many important questions remain unanswered. Some of these will be discussed in this book.

Another aspect of the freedom struggle that is rarely mentioned is the instances of uprisings and mutinies among Indian soldiers in the armies of the East India Company before 1857, and subsequently in the armies of the British Empire. With the exception of the Great Indian Mutiny of 1857, no historian has made more than a passing reference to the revolts and uprisings by personnel of the Armed Forces against British rule. These uprisings occurred throughout the 200 odd years of British rule in India. Many of these revolts were localised to small garrisons, and occurred due to ill-treatment of sepoys by their superiors, racial bias, bad food, abysmal living conditions, apparent injustice, lack of sensitivity to religious or ethnic feelings, etc. However, several revolts were politically motivated and were inspired by a spirit of nationalism, the most prominent being the Great Indian Mutiny of 1857, also called the First War of Indian Independence. Though the mutiny of 1857 was quelled, the spirit of nationalism that it kindled could not be extinguished. A number of smaller mutinies and revolts took place during the next 90 years, especially during the two World Wars and immediately afterwards.

These rebellions played an important role in the decision of the British Government to end colonial rule and grant independence to India in August 1947.

Throughout the history of mankind, kings and chieftains have maintained armies to defend their kingdoms. This was also the case with India, from the earliest times. Even after the arrival of the Mughals and later the British, rulers of smaller kingdoms continued to maintain their own armies which comprised mainly the citizens who fought under the banner of their king. However, it was not uncommon to find soldiers from foreign lands also fighting alongside Indian soldiers. It is important to distinguish the soldier who fights to defend his native land from the mercenary who takes up arms to earn money. A mercenary, also known as a soldier of fortune, is a person who takes up arms for personal profit or reward. Mercenaries fight for money or other forms of payment or for political interests. In the medieval period, mercenaries from the Indo-Gangetic plains, (presently the states of Bihar, Jharkhand and Eastern Uttar Pradesh) known as *Purbias*, were a common feature in kingdoms in Western and Northern India. They were also later recruited by the Marathas and the British. In addition to mercenaries from the Indian subcontinent, Indian rulers often employed those from foreign lands.

In 1498, Vasco da Gama established a sea route to India when he landed at Calicut (now called Kozhikode) on the Malabar Coast. Calicut was a small Hindu Nair kingdom ruled by the Zamorin, who welcomed the Portuguese as traders. Later, he fought several naval wars with Portugal in the 16th century. This was the first modern sea route from Europe to South Asia, and raised Portuguese settlements, which marked the beginning of the colonial era of India. Following in the footsteps of the Portuguese, settlements of the Dutch, French and the British also came up in India. These European interests took centre stage during the colonial wars in India. Travancore became the most dominant state in Kerala by defeating the Zamorin of Calicut in the battle of Purakkad in 1755. After the Dutch were defeated by the Travancore king, Marthanda Varma, the British crown gained control over Kerala through the creation of the Malabar District in northern Kerala and by allying with the newly created princely state of Travancore.

Thousands of Europeans took up service at the courts of rulers all over India. These mercenaries for the most part came from the margins of their respective societies. During the first war between Bahamani Sultanate and Vijayanagara Empire, launched in 1365 by Muhammad Shah I, both sides imported their cannons and employed Turkish and European gunners to man them. European mercenaries served in the courts of Indian rulers for 300 years, beginning with the large-scale defections of Portuguese soldiers from Goa in the 16th century, followed by a series of defections of British soldiers and laymen from the British East India Company settlement at Surat in the 17th century.

When he arrived in India in 1498, Vasco da Gama observed that there were Italian mercenaries in the employ of various *Rajahs* on the Malabar Coast. Two of da Gama's own crewmen had left him to join the Italians in the service of a Malabar *Rajah* for higher wages. According to Portuguese historian João de Barros, there were at least 2,000 Portuguese fighting in the armies of various Indian princes in 1565. The Maratha Chieftain Shivaji employed many Portuguese and hundreds of Goan Catholics and East Indians in his navy, until they were persuaded by the colonial authorities in Goa to desert. They were generally sought after as artillery experts by the Mughals and Marathas. When the Mughals complained to the Portuguese Viceroy António de Melo e Castro about the Portuguese soldiers serving under the Marathas, the latter was forced to respond with a letter stating that he had no control over the Portuguese and native Christian officers in Shivaji's army, just as he had no control over the mercenaries serving in the Mughal and other armies.

There were many mercenaries in the armies of the Deccan sultanates that controlled much of central and southern India. One of the most prominent mercenaries in the Adil Shahi court was Gonçalo Vaz Coutinho, a Portuguese former landowner in Goa, who was imprisoned there on a murder charge before escaping to Bijapur in 1542. There he converted to Islam with his wife and children, and was given grants of lands with large revenues by Ibrahim Adil Shah I. A Portuguese-Jewish gunner, Sancho Pires, defected in similar circumstances to the Ahmadnagar Sultanate in 1530. Pires converted to Islam and took the name Firanghi Khan, acquiring a position of great influence in the Nizam Shahi court.

After Babur's victory over Ibrahim Lodi, the Mewar ruler Rana Sanga led a combined Rajput army of 20,000 intending to defeat Babur and capture Delhi. The Mughals had superior artillery, which prevailed against the Rajput cavalry. It is said that Rana Sanga was betrayed by Raja Shiladitya, also called Silhadi, a Rajput chieftain of northeast Malwa who was a vassal of Mewar. He joined the Rajput confederacy with a garrison of several thousand Rajputs, but it is alleged that he betrayed Sanga in later hours of battle resulting in defeat of the confederacy at the Battle of Khanwa (16 March 1527) which was fought for supremacy of Northern India between Rajputs and Mughals.

In the Battle of Haldighati (21 June 1576) between Akbar and Maharana Pratap Singh, the Mughal army was headed by a Rajput, Raja Man Singh of Amber (now Jaipur), and Akbar's son Salim. The Mughal army had 80,000 horsemen, infantry and some elephants. Among the horsemen, 30,000 were Kachwaha Rajput warriors from Amber, and the rest were Uzbeks, Tajiks, Kazakhs, Sayyids and other Turkish tribes. Maharana Pratap had 18,000 horsemen, some elephants and 400 Bhil warriors under Rana Poonja. A small artillery unit was also with him under Hakim Khan Sur. Maharana Pratap reluctantly retreated with the help of his estranged brother Shakti Singh. His legendary horse Chetak was killed in the battle. Later, Pratap organised a small army of Bhil tribals funded by a Jain businessman called Bhamashah and started a guerrilla war against Akbar and defeated him in the Battle of Dewair (1582). He retook large parts of Mewar but could not recapture Chittor. Raja Man Singh of Jaipur has often been censured by other Rajput rulers for taking up arms against a fellow Rajput, Maharana Pratap of Mewar, on behalf of Akbar. He fought several other battles as the Commander-in-Chief of Akbar's army. This included the capture of Kabul, where he remained for several years as the Governor. Man Singh also led expeditions to crush rebellions in Bihar, Bengal and Orissa.

During the 17th century, many British renegades defected to the service of the Mughals and Deccan sultanates. In 1654, more than twenty British East India Company servants deserted Surat in a single mass break-out. In the 1670s, the British authorities uncovered an active network of covert recruiting agents in Bombay. The increasing defections of British soldiers and East India Company servants led Charles II to issue an order calling back all Englishmen in the employ of Indian princes.

Maharaja Ranjit Singh was a Sikh ruler of the Punjab and the Sikh Empire. His father Maha Singh led Sukerchakia, a *misl* within the Sikh Confederacy. Born in 1780 in Gujranwala, Ranjit Singh succeeded his father at the age of 12. He united the Sikh factions into the Sikh Empire and took the title "Maharaja" on 13 April 1801, to coincide with Baisakhi. Lahore was his capital from 1799. In 1802 he conquered Amritsar, a holy city of the Sikh religion. In 1822 Ranjit Singh hired European mercenaries for the first time to train a part of his troops. He modernised his army, creating a military force whose power delayed the eventual British colonisation of Punjab. The Battle of Jamrud in 1837 was a major setback for Ranjit Singh, when his general, Hari Singh Nalwa, was killed, and the Khyber Pass was established as the western limit of the Sikh Empire's influence. Ranjit Singh died in 1839, and his empire crumbled due to internal strife and poor governance by his heirs. After the First Anglo-Sikh War (1845-1846), Punjab effectively ceased to be an independent state. The British Empire annexed the Sikh Empire following the Second Anglo-Sikh War (1848-49).

The British Indian Army was raised to guard the factories of the British East India Company. It was divided into the Presidency armies of Bengal, Madras and Bombay in 1795, following the fall of the French settlement at Pondicherry in 1793. The Dutch trained the Nair Brigade, the military of Travancore. During the Sepoy mutiny of 1857-58 (also called the Great Indian Mutiny), some units of the Bengal Native Infantry and Cavalry revolted against the British East India Company. The rebels received less support than they had expected from members of the Bombay and Madras Armies. A number of atrocities took place, among them the Siege of Cawnpore. In the Mutiny of 1957, Rani Laxmi Bai of Jhansi had employed Afghans to man her artillery. The mutiny ultimately failed because of lack of resources and coordination among the rebels and assistance provided to the British by Sikhs and Gurkhas. Reprisals by the victorious British Army, assisted by Sikh and Afghan regulars and irregulars, were ruthless.

Following the Sepoy Mutiny, British rule in India was reorganised under the British Raj, made up of areas directly administered by the United Kingdom and princely states under the control of the British Crown, which became the paramount power. Under terms of treaties with the Crown, these princely states were allowed some local autonomy in exchange for protection and representation in international affairs by the United Kingdom. The Raj included present-day India, Pakistan, and Bangladesh. The Presidency Armies were abolished in favour of a reconstituted British Indian Army under the control of the British Crown and the Viceroy. Many units were disbanded or reorganised, and new units of Sikhs, Gurkhas, and irregular horsemen were introduced. The majority of the Madras Native Infantry and Cavalry had their class compositions changed to North Indian tribes, considered more martial than the darker, shorter *"madrassis"* who made up the majority of the Madras Presidency Army. Recruiting focused more on Sikhs and Gurkhas, whom the British viewed as loyal. New caste-based and religion-based regiments were formed.

The British Indian Army consisted of members of all the major religious groups in India: Hindus, Sikhs, Christians, and Muslims. Due to their active participation in the Mutiny, the number of *purbias* from Northern and Eastern states who had earlier formed the bulk of the Bengal Army was reduced. The number of Sikhs in the army grew steadily with time as British commanders came to believe they were more loyal and martial, an impression reinforced by their conduct during the Sepoy Mutiny. The Sikhs, for their part, aligned with the British to prevent a resurgence of Mughal rule, under whom they had been persecuted.

It is interesting to reflect on the reasons for the success of the Mughals and later the British in their success in establishing their rule on almost the entire subcontinent. In both cases, one of the prime reasons for their victories was their ability to exploit the differences between local rulers, with promises of rewards. While the soldiers who fought to defend their kingdoms under the banner of their king did so from a sense of duty, what about those who bore arms against their compatriots under the flag of the ruler of a different state? Were they just mercenaries or did so from a sense of duty when commanded by their rulers?

One of the most well-known cases of treachery occurred on 23 June 1757, in the infamous Battle of Plassey, where British Forces under Robert Clive were able to defeat the troops of Nawab Siraj-ud-Daulah whose trusted commander of the army, Mir Jafar, betrayed his master. Before the battle, Clive had bought Mir Jafar's support through the promise of Siraj-ud-Daulah's crown. No wonder, Mir Jafar is one of the most well-known names in India, for his role in helping the British to gain a foothold in India.

Another Indian prince who falls in this category is Jayajirao Scindia of Gwalior. During the 1857 Mutiny, he preferred to sit on the fence instead of supporting the British or the rebels. Despite his efforts to keep his army on a tight leash, a large segment of his troops responded to the clarion call of the revolutionaries. When asked for help of refuge for rest and recovery by leaders such as Rao Sahib, Jayajirao was egged on by the de facto power holders of Gwalior—Dinkar Rao and Sir Robert Hamilton, to use this opportunity to capture the Rani of Jhansi, Laxmi Bai herself. In an open confrontation at Morar, Scindia realised he was misled about the strength of the rebel forces, and narrowly managed to escape capture. Much later, when a battered Laxmi Bai, left with few options, approached him again for help, he granted her the same but betrayed her again by alerting the British. In an attempted cover-up, he then let the queen escape with a weak horse, knowing that she would finally fall.

For Tatya Tope, the rebellion turned personal when Nana Saheb the beloved Maratha aristocrat fell victim to the loathed 'Doctrine of Lapse'. The Raja of Narwar, Mann Singh, became an easy target of the British's 'divide and rule' policy. In return for aiding the capture of Tatya Tope, the

Raja was promised the return of his lost *jagir*, at Gwalior. So Mann Singh pretended to invite Tatya Tope for advice regarding a potential political alliance with Firoze Shah against the British. After their discussions, when Tatya Tope lay down to rest, he was pinned down by the Raja's soldiers, shackled and handed over to the British.

Were the Indian soldiers in the armies of the East India Company and the British Raj mercenaries? This question has often been debated, but seldom answered satisfactorily. It should be remembered that the British came to India not as invaders but as traders. After the grant of the *diwani* by the Mughal Emperor, the East India Company acquired the status of a vassal, with the authority to collect revenue on behalf of the Mughal Empire. To facilitate this responsibility they were permitted to maintain an army. The sepoys serving in the Company's army had a position similar to that of soldiers in the armies of local rajas and chieftains. Even after the assumption of power by the British Crown, the status of the sepoy did not change. Military service during the British Raj was considered an honourable profession, and much sought after. Though native states maintained their own armies, they were not on par with that of the British Raj. India as a nation did not exist at that time, and it was the British Indian Army which fulfilled the role of a national army, whose primary task was to defend India against external attack. In the early part of the twentieth century, as the struggle for freedom gained momentum, many Indian soldiers and officers were imbued with nationalistic feelings. Nevertheless, they continued to serve since they did not see any conflict between military service and nationalism. Significantly, political leaders such as Bal Gangadhar Tilak, Lala Lajpat Rai, Mahatma Gandhi and Motilal Nehru held similar views. It is interesting to note that many soldiers with nationalistic feelings contemplated leaving the service and joining the freedom struggle, especially in the 1930s and early 1940s. However, when they sought the advice of political leaders, they were invariably discouraged from taking such a step.

A noteworthy event that occurred during World War II was the birth of the Indian National Army (INA), a Japanese-sponsored force created from

Indian prisoners of war. Many of those who joined the INA claimed they did so for patriotic reasons, and refute the charges of treason—as the act of going over to the enemy is regarded in the army—by arguing that after the fall of Singapore, they were handed over to the Japanese authorities by the British, who thereafter had no claim on their allegiance. This is a strange argument, since after every mass surrender, the senior captured officer hands over charge of the men under this command to the victor. This is what Percival did after the fall of Singapore in 1942 and Niazi after the fall of Dacca in 1971. The act of being handed over to the enemy is a military custom, which does not absolve the captured soldiers from their allegiance or duty. It is also worth remembering that India was then at war with Japan, and joining the enemy to fight one's own compatriots could hardly be termed a patriotic act. This was realised by the leaders of the freedom struggle, who denounced the INA in no uncertain terms Most Indian leaders, including Gandhi, trusted the British more than the Japanese, having heard of the atrocities committed by the latter in China. They surmised that Japanese rule over India would be decidedly worse than that of the British, which in any case was about to end. Most important of all, they wanted to gain freedom on their own, not with the help of a foreign power.

Though Subhas Chandra Bose was a popular figure, the activities of the INA remained practically unknown until the end of World War II. It was the Red Fort trials that brought them into the limelight, thanks to the Congress, which found another reason to mobilise public opinion against British rule. Having opposed the INA during the War, Congress leaders suddenly changed their stand, and promptly formed a defence team that included prominent lawyers such as Bhulabhai Desai, Asaf Ali, Jawaharlal Nehru, Tej Bahadur Sapru, Kailash Nath Katju and others. The Indian Armed Forces could not remain unaffected by this change, and opinions differed widely regarding the treatment of those who had broken their oath of loyalty. Many felt that the soldiers who joined the INA had been untrue to their salt and deserved no sympathy, while others were of the opinion that they were genuine patriots, even if the methods adopted by them were wrong. This is often quoted as the reason for the mutinies that occurred in the three armed services early in 1946. A close examination reveals that the root causes of the three mutinies were discrimination between British and Indian soldiers in matters of pay, food, accommodation, along with resentment against the harsh punishments awarded to the INA prisoners. Based on this, many INA veterans claim a major share of the credit for obtaining freedom from British rule. However, this argument is fallacious, since the INA had ceased to exist when these mutinies occurred. The mutineers were protesting against the British action taken against the INA personnel, which they felt was too harsh. However, this does not indicate that they condoned the actions of the men in joining INA and fighting alongside Japan, an enemy country. In fact, the feeling against them in the Indian Army was so strong that the Commander-in-Chief, Field Marshal Auchinleck, had to issue strict instructions to ensure the safety of the INA personnel who had become prisoners after the fall of Rangoon.

There are several other reasons for not upholding the claim of the INA of having contributed significantly to India's independence. None of the persons in authority who were responsible for the decision—Attlee, Pethick-Lawrence, Cripps, Wavell, or Mountbatten—acknowledged or mentioned that the INA played a part in their discussions. The same applies to the leaders of the freedom struggle, such as Gandhi, Nehru, Jinnah and many others. On the other hand, there is ample evidence to prove that the Indian Armed Forces figured prominently in the deliberations that preceded the end of British rule in India. Having forsaken their allegiance to the Indian Army by joining the Japanese, INA personnel could not be treated as members of the Indian Army, unlike the other prisoners of war who elected to undergo hard labour and torture rather break their oath of loyalty.

Though Indian soldiers, sailors and airmen continued to serve with commitment until the end, it would be wrong to assume that they did so willingly. The wave of nationalistic fervour sweeping through the country forced many of them to introspect their role in the freedom struggle, leaving some confused and insecure. The men naturally looked to their officers for guidance, who were equally uncertain about their future course of action.

These issues, coupled with the growing aspirations for independence, became a source of concern for the military hierarchy, which was aware of the discontent and alienation of Indian officers. They tried to take remedial measures, but it was too late. By the time World War II ended, Indian officers had become true nationalists.

Most people in India, and indeed the World, believe that the chief architect of independence was Mahatma Gandhi, who left the British rulers bewildered with his new weapon—non-violence—against which they had no defence. This may be the truth, but not the whole truth. Irrespective of official pronouncements from the Viceroy's House on Raisina Hill in Delhi or Whitehall in London, the British were loath to leave India, right up to the end of 1946. Even as the Cabinet Mission was trying to reconcile the differences between the Congress and Muslim League, the Chiefs of Staff in London were examining options to continue their hold on India. After rejecting options involving withdrawal from India for strategic reasons, they proceeded to work out the quantum of British troops that were required to keep the country under control, since the Indian Armed Forces could no longer be trusted. At one stage, the British Government seriously considered a recruitment drive in Europe to raise the additional troops needed for this purpose. It was only after they failed to find the five British divisions that Auchinleck had asked for that they agreed, very reluctantly, to quit India. Had the Indian Armed Forces, especially the Army, remained staunch, there is little doubt that British rule would have continued for at least another 10 to 15 years. The nationalistic feeling that had entered the heart of the Indian soldier was one of the most important factors in the British decision to grant complete independence to India, and also to advance the date from June 1948 to August 1947.

Soon after the end of the war in 1945, there were three prominent uprisings in the Armed Services in 1946. These were the mutinies in the RIN (Royal Indian Navy), RIAF (Royal Indian Air Force) and the Army Signals Training Centre in Jubbulpore, as it was then known. All these occurred at almost the same time in early 1946. Strangely enough, the Naval mutiny was well publicised, compared to the others. This is ironical since it was the unrest in the Army that caused them the most concern, as is clear from the deliberations and correspondence between the British authorities in India and Britain. At that time, the RIN and RIAF were miniscule forces, whereas the Indian Army was one of the largest military forces in the World. It had played a major role in the victory of the Allied Powers in World War I and II. In fact, it was the most vital instrument of power the British had to control their empire not only in India but in almost all countries in South East Asia.

As a matter of fact, it was the Army mutiny in Jubbulpore that was largely instrumental in the British decision to quit India in 1947. However, very little has been written about this important event. In fact, though the Corps of Signals was his parent arm, the author himself was not conversant with the details of the mutiny and its effects during his service. It was only after he retired and began work on the History of the Corps of Signals, Volume II, covering the period from the outbreak of World War II in 1939 to the grant of Independence in 1947, that he was able to study the documents that exist in the Signals Museum and the Signals Records in Jabalpur, as well as those in the History Division of the Ministry Defence. As a result of his research, details of the mutiny in the Signals Training Centre at Jubbulpore were included for the first time in the regimental history of the Corps of Signals. The author was also able to do a research project on the subject under the aegis of the Centre for Armed Forces Historical Research in the United Service Institution of India (USI), which resulted in the publication of the book titled, *Contribution of the Armed Forces to the Freedom Movement in India*. Some portions of this have been used in the present publication.

2
The Naval Mutiny—1946

When World War II started in September 1939 the Royal Indian Navy was a miniscule force, consisting of about 1,500 sailors and 150 officers. By the time the War ended, its strength had multiplied almost fifteen times. In December 1945, it had 2,438 officers, 214 warrant officers and 21,193 ratings. During the war, there were several mutinies in the service. In March 1942, ratings at the Mechanics Training Establishment at Bombay mutinied demanding higher pay, resulting in seven being sentenced to three months imprisonment. In June 1942 the ratings of HMIS *Konkan*, which was then in the UK, went on hunger strike, due to problems connected with food, accommodation and the scale of rations. Seventeen sailors were awarded three months rigorous imprisonment. Three months later, there was a major case of insubordination on board the HMIS *Orissa*, again in the UK. This time, not only the men but also the officers were punished. The Commanding Officer was tried by a general court martial and sentenced to lose a year's seniority. The 2nd officer and the gunnery officer also lost three months' seniority. Thirteen ratings were discharged, and awarded imprisonment terms ranging from three to seven years. Almost at the same time, there was a less serious case of indiscipline on the HMIS *Khyber* in the UK, after which three men were discharged.

After the four cases in 1942, there were no revolts for almost two years, when there were several incidents with religious overtones. In June 1944, Muslim sailors of the HMIS *Akbar* in Bombay revolted, demanding a mosque, resulting in the discharge of 100 Pathans. A month later, Muslim sailors on board the HMIS *Hamlawar* at Bombay assaulted a sub-lieutenant, alleging that he had insulted the Koran. The officer was found guilty and lost three months' seniority. Thirteen men were discharged and ten sentenced to varying terms of imprisonment. In July 1944 the men on board HMIS *Shivaji* at Lonavla refused to eat meat that they suspected was contaminated with pork and four had to be discharged. In March 1945 three men on board HMIS *Himalaya* in Karachi went to a mosque after being refused permission. They were declared absent without leave and sentenced to a year's rigorous imprisonment. A month later, there was another revolt on the HMIS *Shivaji* when 51 ratings refused to clean the ship. Thirty-eight were awarded three months rigorous imprisonment.[1]

After the end of World War II, the bulk of the Royal Indian Navy was located at Bombay, with smaller complements at Karachi, Madras, Calcutta, Vizagapatnam, Cochin and several other stations. The establishment at Bombay comprised the Royal Indian Navy Depot, which included the Castle Barracks that housed about 900 ratings awaiting appointment to ships or shore establishments; the Fort Barracks that housed the HO (Hostilities Only) ratings; the CCO (Central Communications Office) that handled all signal traffic at Bombay; the Colaba Receiving Station; the Mahul Wireless Station in Trombay Island and the RIN Hospital at Sewri. The other shore establishments at Bombay were HMIS *Talwar*, the training school for communication ratings; HMIS *Machlimar* at Versova, the anti-submarine training school; HMIS *Hamla* at Marve that held the landing craft; HMIS *Kakauri*, the demobilisation centre that held about 1,400 ratings; HMIS *Cheetah*, the second demobilisation centre and training school for Special Service ratings; and HMIS *Feroze* on Malabar Hill that functioned as a training school and demobilisation centre for officers. There was a large number of ships: HMIS *Narbada* and *Jumna* (sloops); *Dhanush* and *Shamsher* (frigates); *Gondwana, Assam, Mahratta* and *Sind* (corvettes); *Kumaon, Kathiawar, Khyber, Punjab, Bombay, Madras, Orissa* and *Oudh* (minesweepers); *Clive* and *Lawrence* (old sloops); *Agra, Cuttack, Karachi, Lahore, Madura, Nautilus, Nasik, Patna, Poona, Rampur, Berar, Amritsar,* and *Cochin* (trawlers); *Nilam, Moti, Lal* and *Heera* (Persian gun boats); *Kalawati, Ramdas, Dipawati* and *Bhadrawati* (auxiliary vessels) and a few motor minesweepers. All the ships and establishments were involved in the mutiny, the lone exception being the Frigate HMIS *Shamsher*.[2]

One of the important establishments at Bombay was the HMIS *Talwar*, the Communication Ratings Training School. When World War II ended, the *Talwar* was under the command of Lieutenant Commander E.M. Shaw. In September 1945, Shaw was transferred as Staff Communication Officer, being relieved by Lieutenant Commander A.T.J. Cole. Both Shaw and Cole were experienced officers and popular with the men. At that time, apart from the 200 communication ratings there were about 700 men under training and about 300 ratings of the draft reserve awaiting demobilisation, housed in the *Talwar*. As a result, there was an accommodation crunch. Though the number of ratings was fairly large, there were very few officers. The overcrowding in the barracks, with a large number of men having nothing to do, and an almost complete lack of supervision, all contributed to the dissatisfaction and unrest. On 30 November 1945, on the eve of Navy Day, slogans such as 'Quit India', 'Revolt Now', 'Kill the White Dogs' and 'Down with the Imperialists' were found written on walls. An inquiry was held but the perpetrators could not be traced. However, a rating named Deb was suspected and discharged on grounds of "services no longer required".[3]

On 21 January 1946, HMIS *Talwar* got a new commanding officer, Commander F. W. King. Like many British officers in the Royal Indian Navy at that time, King had never served in India earlier and was unfamiliar with the customs, castes and religious prejudices that are so important in this country. The appointment of King was resented by the ship's company, especially since he was not a Communication Officer, and known for his rough treatment of ratings. It was generally believed that King was sent to the *Talwar* to set things in order since his predecessor, Cole, was lenient and regarded as pro-Indian. On 1 February 1946, slogans similar to those that had been seen two months earlier reappeared on a platform on the *Talwar* from which the Commander-in-Chief was to take the salute on the next day. The originator, Leading Telegraphist B.C. Dutt was caught and placed under close arrest. However, the slogans continued and one day the tyres of the Commanding Officer's car were deflated. A few anonymous letters addressed to Commander King also reached his office.

The incident that triggered the mutiny occurred on 8 February 1946 when Commander King entered the barrack where several off-duty ratings from the Central Communications Office were resting after having finished their breakfast. Reportedly, King heard some catcalls from the barrack at some WRINs (Women's Royal Indian Navy) who were passing by, and was annoyed by the uncivilised behaviour of the ratings, who he thought were abstaining from duty. The men did not notice his presence and continued talking, instead of coming to their feet and paying compliments to the Commanding Officer. King lost his temper and lashed out at the men, using abusive terms such as 'sons of bitches', *'junglees'* and 'coolies', before stomping out of the barrack. The men were agitated, and the next day, fourteen ratings put in a complaint against Commander King for using foul language. On 9 February 1946, a Saturday, they were seen by Lieutenant Commander Shaw, who told them that he would forward their complaint to the Commanding Officer. On Monday, Shaw informed King, who agreed to see the men next Saturday, the day on which personal interviews were granted. Shaw tried to impress upon King that in view of the seriousness and urgency of the matter, it would be better to see them earlier and not wait until Saturday, but the latter did not agree. When King saw the men, he warned them that it was a serious offence to make a false complaint against a senior officer. In accordance with regulations, he would give them 24 hours to think over the matter, after which they could, if they wished, put their request in writing. On the same day, Dutt was summarily tried, and a report sent to Naval Headquarters. The ratings did exactly what they were told to do, presenting their written complaints on the morning of 18 February. By this time, the mutiny had already broken out.

The situation on HMIS *Talwar* had worsened during the week, and all that was needed was a spark to ignite the fire. On 17 February 1946, a Sunday, cooks in two vegetarian messes mixed *dal* (lentils) and vegetables for the evening meal, which the men refused to eat, complaining that it was tasteless and unpalatable. The duty officer came to know of the incident, but did not report it. The ratings went to bed hungry, but did not create any trouble. Next morning, a large number of men refused to eat breakfast and shouted slogans. King was informed when he reached his office at about 9 a.m., but he left soon afterwards to have his breakfast, without leaving any instructions. He returned to his office after about half an hour. When divisions were piped, Indian ratings did not come to the parade ground and began shouting and jeering. The Flag Officer Bombay was informed on telephone that the men were not listening to the officers and were completely out of control. King held a conference that was attended by all officers and warrant officers. However, no plans were made or instructions given for dealing with the situation. Lieutenants S.N. Kohli and S.M. Nanda—both were destined to become Chiefs of Naval Staff—volunteered to act as trouble-shooters and made another attempt to speak to the men. However, they were hooted down.[4]

At midday, the Flag Officer Bombay, Rear Admiral A.R. Rattray, arrived and spoke to the men, asking them to return to duty and then left. However, the men did not obey his orders, and the situation worsened. By this time all other establishments that were manned by communication ratings had been affected. This included the Central Communication Office that was manned by ratings from the *Talwar*, as well as the Receiving Station at Colaba and the Dockyard Signal Station. B.C. Dutt, who was under detention, was sent by King to try and pacify the deserters, but they were in no mood to listen. In the evening at about 5 p.m. Admiral Rattray again visited HMIS *Talwar* and spoke to the men. He asked them to appoint representatives who should meet him next morning with the list of grievances. He also informed them that Commander King was being replaced by Captain Inigo-Jones. This only added fuel to the fire, since Inigo-Jones was known for his anti-Indian bias and repressive measures, an example of which he had exhibited when dealing with a similar outbreak at the Mechanical Training Establishment, resulting in him being given the pseudonym "butcher of the RIN".[5]

On 19 February, Rear Admiral Rattray arrived at about 9.30 a.m. and met the representatives of the ratings. However, by this time some ratings from other establishments had also arrived and a few of them tried to disrupt the meeting. The ratings handed over to Rattray a list of 14 demands, as given below:

- No victimisation.
- Release of RK Singh, who had been detained earlier.
- Speeding up demobilisation.
- Action against Commander King.
- Improvement in the standard of food.
- Indian ratings to be given the same scale of pay and allowances as personnel of the Royal Navy, along with access to NAAFI canteens.
- Kit not to be taken back at the time of release.
- Grant of higher terminal benefits on release.
- Good behaviour by officers towards ratings.
- Regular promotion of lower deck personnel as officers.
- Appointment of a new Commanding Officer.
- Immediate release of INA prisoners and Captain Rashid, who had been sentenced to rigorous imprisonment.
- Enquiry into incidents of firing on public all over India.
- Withdrawal of Indian troops from Indonesia and Middle East.[6]

While the first eleven demands pertained to the Navy, the last three were of a political nature, which were probably added as an afterthought. All that Admiral Rattray could do was to assure the men that he would forward their request to the FOCRIN (Flag Officer Commanding Royal Indian Navy) at Delhi. Some ratings had hauled down the Naval Ensign while the meeting was going on, but it was quickly hoisted again. Admiral Rattray left the *Talwar* at about 11.40 a.m., returning at 3.45 p.m. for a second brief visit. By this time the unrest had spread to other establishments in Bombay. About 2,000 ratings came to the breakwater and asked the sailors manning the ships to join a 'sit-down' strike. Some ratings joined a procession in the streets, taken out by ratings from other establishments. This did not go unnoticed and soon everyone in the city came to know of the strike. The news was also broadcast by All India Radio and reached other stations around the country. Accompanied by the Area Commander and the Commissioner, Admiral Rattray visited the *Talwar* again at 10.20 p.m. After spending a few minutes, they left for the Castle Barracks, where the situation appeared to be more serious.

Captain Inigo-Jones was in command of the Castle Barracks up to 19 February 1946 when he was transferred to HMIS *Talwar*, handing over to Commander E.C. Streatfield-James. When the latter arrived at Castle Barracks in the morning at about 8.30 a.m., he found his way barred by several jostling sailors. He forced his way in and held a conference with the men. He had almost succeeded in convincing them to give up the strike when a sailor from another establishment arrived and asked the men to follow him. More than 200 ratings agreed to go with him and left in a procession to the *Talwar*. This was immediately conveyed to the Flag Officer Bombay. Soon after this when some officers arrived and were entering the gates the sailors crowded round them and made them remove their caps, shouting '*topi utaro*'. Most of them complied, but Lieutenant Commander B.S. Soman, who was later to head the Indian Navy, apparently refused, telling them that since he had not put on his cap with the permission of the ratings, he saw no reason to take it off on their orders.[7]

Around midday a sailor hauled down the Ensign, but it was re-hoisted by Lieutenant Sassoon. Commander Streatfield-James tried to open a dialogue with the men but they were in no mood to listen to the Indian officers who were sent to talk to them. Nothing noteworthy happened after this and the men had their lunch as usual. In the evening Streatfield-James went to Vithal House and pleaded with the Flag Officer Bombay for military aid. Later that night, two chief petty officers from Fort Barracks entered Castle Barracks and demanded the release of about 150 sailors who had been arrested in the *bazaar* by the military and police during the day. When this was refused, they left, threatening that they would secure the release of the prisoners by force. At 11 p.m. the Flag Officer Bombay arrived, accompanied by the Area Commander, Major General Beard and Brigadier Southgate. Commander Streatfield-James asked for the Army to be called in, but the Flag Officer Bombay did not agree.

Apart from the *Talwar* and Castle Barracks where the major events occurred on 19 February 1946, there were some incidents on other ships and establishments also. About 250 to 300 ratings from HMIS *Kakaur* broke into HMIS *Machlimar*, shouting slogans. They asked the ratings of the *Machlimar* to join them. Some agreed while a couple of reluctant ratings were forcibly dragged out. Some ratings of HMIS *Assam* hoisted a Congress flag and refused work in sympathy with the ratings of the *Talwar*. They also took out some weapons and indulged in looting.

Seeing the Congress flag flying on the *Assam* the sailors of HMIS *Sind* and HMIS *Mahratta* also refused work. On HMIS *Shivaji* flags of both the Congress and the Muslim League were hoisted and the ratings shouted slogans such as 'Quit India' and 'Quit Indonesia'. On HMIS *Clive* the communication branch ratings went on strike, with six leading telegraphists and forty-six ordinary telegraphists refusing to turn out. The HMIS *Punjab* and HMIS *Berar* were in the dockyard. A crowd of about 2,000 ratings appeared on the breakwater and boarded both ships, pulling down the Ensigns and the Union Jacks. The ratings of the ships did not join them but refused work.

On 20 February 1946 at about 2 a.m. a party of 150 sailors from HMIS *Hamla* forced their way into the Castle Barracks, led by Lieutenant Sobhani, who had joined the striking ratings. Sobhani asked the ratings in Castle Barracks to join him and left after twenty minutes. Streatfield-James immediately called for military aid. The Area Commander, in consultation with the Flag Officer Bombay, decided to place a platoon each at the Central Communication Office, Colaba Receiving Station and Mahaul Wireless Station. At 6 a.m. a platoon of the Mahratta Light Infantry (MLI) arrived. Two hours later a lorry full of ratings drove inside the Castle Barracks. All hands were called to the quarterdeck where a spokesman addressed them. They were informed that a Central Strike Committee had been formed with Leading Seaman M.S. Khan as the President and Petty Officer (Telegraphist) Madan Singh as the Vice President. The ratings of Castle Barracks were asked to elect two representatives for the Central Strike Committee, who were later taken to the *Talwar* in the lorry.

The FOCRIN (Flag Officer Commanding Royal Indian Navy), Vice Admiral J.H. Godfrey flew down to Bombay from Delhi in the morning. After consulting the Flag Officer Bombay and General Rob Lockhart, the GOC-in-C Southern Command, he agreed that help from the military was essential to quell the unrest. Before returning to Delhi the FOCRIN met some members of the Strike Committee, led by Leading Seaman Khan.

At about 2.30 p.m. two additional platoons of the MLI arrived at Castle Barracks, bringing up their strength to a company. Some of the ratings threw stones at the troops, who soon established machine gun posts to cover the entry and exit gates. About 150 ratings were arrested outside Castle Barracks. In the afternoon at 4 p.m. M.S. Khan, the president of the Strike Committee, arrived and addressed the men. Soon afterwards the men watched a cinema show that had been organised for the ratings. Things were relatively quiet until 6.30 p.m. when the ratings who were outside returned and demanded that the troops be withdrawn. The situation appeared to be worsening but the troops maintained their cool and did not fire.

The situation on *Talwar* seemed to be calm until about 2.45 p.m. when troops from the MLI arrived and were posted at the gates. A sailor who wanted to go out was prevented from doing so, leading to some violence that subsided after the guard fired one shot. A crowd of about 300 ratings broke into the *Machlimar*, hauled down the White Ensign, tore it up and hoisted a 'Jai Hind' flag. They damaged vehicles and broke window-panes. When they left, all ratings joined them. On *Clive* the seamen and stokers also joined the telegraphists, who had mutinied the previous day. They took over a motor boat that was used to ferry them ashore.

The mutiny reached its peak on 21 February 1946, a day that was characterised by violence and high drama. In the morning some of the mutineers in Castle Barracks asked for permission to go to the *Talwar*, to contact their leaders and get instructions. They were given transport and left at about 7.30 a.m. They returned after some time and told the others that it has been decided that the strike will continue. At about 9 a.m. the ratings tried to force their way out of the main gate. A crowd of civilians and ratings had gathered near the gate. The commander of the guard, a British major, warned them but when this did not have any effect, he ordered the guard to open fire. The MLI troops were reluctant to fire on the ratings and this resulted in some delay before they were opened fire. The troops fired one round each, and a total of 18 rounds in all were fired, most of them directed not at the ratings but at the ground in front of them. The ratings immediately closed the gate, placed motor vehicles across it, rushed back towards the barracks, broke open the armoury and took out weapons and ammunition. Soon they were firing back at the troops from the ramparts.

The military cordoned off the area around the Castle Barracks and cleared the roads passing along the Mint and Town Hall. All offices and establishments were closed and the workers who arrived for work were turned back. The MLI platoons were replaced by troops of the Leicestershire Regiment. British troops and Royal Marines were deployed to guard all approaches to Castle Barracks and the waterfront at the Gateway of India. The firing from Castle Barracks intensified and one RAF airman in the CCO was injured. In addition to rifles, the ratings began using light machine guns and grenades. The firing continued for almost six hours and ceased only when a 'ceasefire' came into effect later in the day.

The sound of firing was heard by the men aboard the ships, who were all on the decks, looking anxiously towards the Castle Barracks from where messages were being transmitted informing them of the firing. At about 10.30 a.m. M.S. Khan, the President of the Strike Committee, came to the bridge of the *Kumaon* and addressed the men. Speaking in both Urdu and English he exhorted the men to raise steam, load guns and stand by for action. He warned the men that they might have to take up battle positions to defend themselves and the dockyard. He also asked them to order all British officers to leave their ships, asserting that the ratings could do without them. Indian officers could also leave, in case they wished to. His inflammatory speech had the desired effect, and the men promptly armed themselves with whatever weapons they could lay their hands on. The officers were ordered to hand over the keys to magazines and leave the ships. In the flagship of the RIN, the *Narbada*, the ratings did not bother to ask for the keys—they simply broke open the magazine and loaded the guns.

Around midday the CCO was evacuated and control of Castle Barracks was handed over to the Army. However, five naval officers, including two medical officers in the Depot Sick Quarters, were trapped inside. After some rough treatment at the hands of the ratings, they were permitted to leave in the evening. Surgeon Lieutenant Commander Martin, the Senior Medical Officer, offered to talk to the Flag Officer Bombay and arrange for a truce. The ratings were initially suspicious but later agreed. Martin spoke to Commander Payne at Vithal House, who informed him that they had already contacted the Central Strike Committee, which was planning to send a truce party to Castle Barracks.

The situation in *Talwar* became tense after the firing in Castle Barracks. At about 10 a.m. Captain Inigo-Jones, accompanied by Leading Seaman Khan and two other members of the Strike Committee, left for Castle Barracks to persuade the ratings to stop firing. Jones returned alone after an hour, leading to excitement and rumours that persisted until Khan came back in the evening. At 2.20 p.m. the FOCRIN broadcast a message on All India Radio, which was relayed to all ships at 5.45 p.m. He ended his broadcast with the chilling message:

> ... I want again to make it quite plain that the Government of India will never give in to violence. To continue the struggle is the height of folly when you take into account the overwhelming forces at the disposal of the Government at this time and which will be used to their utmost even if it means the destruction of the Navy of which we have been so proud.[8]

After the firing at Castle Barracks, the situation was critical because there was a grave danger of the ships under control of the mutineers opening fire on the city and causing casualties to civilians. Some ships did open fire with machine guns and Oerlikons in the direction of Castle Barracks but fortunately there was little effect. In some cases, the weapons were being manned by untrained personnel such as ship's clerks, cooks and wireless operators who had never handled them before. Due to lack of coordination and communication there was considerable confusion and a spate of rumours. This sometimes resulted in comic situations, such as the one concerning HMIS *Kumaon*, which was moored adjacent to the breakwater and being used by the Central Strike Committee for its deliberations. After Khan came on board and addressed the men, the officers left the ship. The Oerlikon was loaded and the ship put out to sea. However, after sailing about 100 feet it returned and was secured.

After the call for the officers to leave their ships most of them were allowed to go after handing over their weapons. Some of the Indian officers remained on board, but stayed below decks. In most cases, the officers left without any difficulty, the ratings themselves assisting them. Meanwhile, the FOCRIN asked the Commander-in-Chief East Indies to send a naval force to assist in putting down the mutiny. In London, Prime Minister Attlee informed the House of Commons that several warships including a cruiser of the Royal Navy were speeding towards Bombay in response to an urgent request from India. Overall command of the situation was now in the hands of Lieutenant General Rob Lockhart, GOC-in-C Southern Command, who had received instructions from the Commander-in-Chief, General Claude Auchinleck. By the evening a regiment of artillery equipped with 12-pounder guns, two British infantry battalions and several armoured cars had reached the city. RAF bombers had already arrived at Santa Cruz and the cruiser *Glasgow* was expected soon from Trincomalee.

Sardar Vallabhbhai Patel, a member of the Congress Working Committee, was in Bombay at that time. The mutineers contacted him and requested his help. But Sardar Patel refused to interfere, making it clear that it was wrong on their part to take up arms against their superiors. He termed it as an act of indiscipline, which could not be condoned in an armed service like the Navy. This was a setback to the mutineers, who had been counting on the support of the political leaders. The ultimatum in the FOCRIN's broadcast also dampened their spirits, and many started having second thoughts about the strike. At 4.30 p.m. Khan sent a message to all ships to cease fire and await further instructions, which would be communicated after his meeting with the FOCRIN and Flag Officer Bombay. In the evening a truce party of officers visited the Castle Barracks and told them to give up their arms since talks were now going on between the government and the national leaders, and the matter would be resolved soon. The ratings were reluctant to surrender their arms but agreed when they were informed that this would result in loss of support from the political parties. Eventually they decided to hand over the weapons and ammunition and release the detained officers.

By dusk the firing had stopped but the troops were not withdrawn. The supply of food and water had also not been restored. It was made clear to the mutineers that troops would be withdrawn only after they surrendered unconditionally. The Strike Committee met in the *Talwar* to review the situation and decide its next move. It drew up an appeal to the people and all political parties to come to their aid. Drawing attention to their demands and the brutal methods being adopted by the authorities to crush their 'peaceful strike', they called for a *hartal* (general strike). Pointing to the threat of the FOCRIN to destroy the Indian Navy, the Committee said:

> You do not want your Indian brothers to be destroyed by British bullets. You know our demands are just, you must support us. We appeal to you all, particularly to the leaders of the Congress, League and Communist parties: Use all your might to prevent a blood bath in Bombay! Force the naval authorities to stop shooting and threats and to negotiate with us! Rally our people to support us, through a peaceful hartal and peaceful strikes! We appeal to you, brothers and sisters, to respond.[9]

On 22 February 1946 the situation remained critical, and incidents of looting and hooliganism continued. At about 10 a.m. the FOCRIN arrived at HMIS *Talwar* and was received outside the gate by Captain Inigo-Jones. Shortly afterwards command of *Talwar* was handed over to Commander S.G. Karmakar. The Wireless Telegraphy station at Mahul was handed over to the Army. At about 11 a.m. a message from the FOCRIN was delivered to the mutineers over a loud hailer, informing them that the C-in-C Southern Command has assumed control in

Bombay. To show them that ample forces were available in Bombay, the C-in-C had ordered a formation of RAF aircraft to fly over the harbour in the afternoon. The aircraft would not take any offensive action, provided no action was taken against them. If the mutineers decided to surrender, they were to hoist a black or blue flag and muster all hands on deck on the side facing Bombay and await further orders. At about 2.30 p.m. a formation of bombers flew over the harbour.

The citizens of Bombay had shown their sympathy with the ratings from the day the strike began. On 19 February, the people were amazed to see the ratings parading through the streets, shouting slogans. Many of them cheered the ratings and some even joined the processions. The spectacle was repeated next morning, with larger crowds watching and cheering the ratings. The same afternoon troops were positioned at the gates of the naval barracks. A large crowd collected outside and many of them passed on food packets to the ratings confined inside. On 21 February, when the situation escalated and the ratings attacked the guards, the civilian crowd joined them. The firing by the guards caused considerable excitement in the city and a large crowd collected around the Gateway of India and several other places. In many places there were scenes of hooliganism and looting, and the Police had to open fire to control the mobs. By the evening, the people came to know of the Strike Committee's call for a *hartal* the next day. In spite of Sardar Patel's appeal not to observe the *hartal*, many people responded. Among them were 30,000 millhands who downed tools, as well as workers in other establishments such as offices, workshops and tramway depots. The city transport system collapsed and unruly crowds attacked Europeans at several places, setting fire to their shops, offices and cars. The situation was beyond the control of the Police and British troops were brought in to restore order. The crowds placed barricades on roads to impede the movement of military vehicles and resorted to violence, leading to fire being opened at several places. Finally, curfew had to be imposed in the dockyard and the adjoining areas.

Sardar Patel, whom the mutineers had met a day earlier, sent the following message to the mutineers:

The strikers should lay down all arms and should go through the formality of a surrender and the Congress would do its level best to see that there is no victimization and the legitimate demands of Naval ratings are met as soon as possible.[10]

Because of the curfew imposed during the previous night, the city appeared calm in the morning on 23 February 1946. But, as the day advanced, crowds began to collect on the streets. The newspapers carried the news that the strike had been called off at the instance of Sardar Patel and Jinnah, but most people refused to believe this and took to the streets. During the day, violence occurred at several places in the heavily populated working-class areas. Rioters looted shops selling food grains and textiles, and set fire to factories, including the Kohinoor and Usha Woollen Mills. The entire city seemed to be in flames, with hundreds of motor cars, buses, trams and train coaches being set on fire. A three thousand strong crowd attacked the Police Station at Mahim, and almost lynched the Inspector in charge. The living quarters of policemen were ransacked at Two Tanks and Null Bazaar and their belongings thrown on the streets. Clashes between the rioters and the Police and Military left about 150 people dead and over 1,500 injured. Citizens recalled that this was the worst rioting that the city had witnessed in living memory.

As the day wore on the pressure on the leaders of the mutiny increased to resolve the impasse. The shortage of food and water had begun to tell on their endurance. The stern warning from the authorities, the military presence and the snub from the political leaders left them with little choice. The Central Strike Committee met on *Talwar* and deliberated on the message received from Sardar Patel. Without the support of the Congress, they realised that they could not achieve anything and it was decided to call off the strike. There were many who did not agree, and wanted to carry on the struggle. Shortly afterwards, a message arrived from Jinnah that echoed the advice given by Patel, asking them to surrender, and promising to see that justice was done. At 4.30 p.m. representatives of all ships were brought to the *Talwar* and met the Strike Committee, which apprised them of this decision. At 6.15 p.m., the representatives informed Commodore Karmakar that they were ready to surrender unconditionally. The information was conveyed to all other stations and ships outside Bombay. The mutiny was over.

Other than Bombay, the station most affected by the mutiny was Karachi. Though the number of ships and establishments was smaller, in terms of violence and casualties Karachi surpassed Bombay. The mutiny affected the two ships that were anchored in the harbour at Keamari—HMIS *Hindustan* and HMIS *Travancore*—and the three shore establishments at Manora—HMIS *Bahadur*, the Boys' Training Establishment; HMIS *Chamak*, the Radar School and HMIS *Himalaya*, the Gunnery School. All the ships and establishments were affected with the *Hindustan* witnessing the heaviest exchange of fire between the mutineers and troops of the Indian Army. When the mutiny ended at Karachi on 23 February 1946, eight lives had been lost and 33 persons lay wounded, including some British soldiers.

The mutiny in Bombay started on 19 February but it was only on the next day that the effect was felt in Karachi. Since the mutiny had been initiated by ratings from the communication branch in Bombay, it was easy for them to convey the information to their colleagues manning communications in other ships and establishments. However, the signal that triggered the mutiny at Karachi came not from Bombay but from Delhi. At about 10 a.m. a message was received from Naval Headquarters ordering HMIS *Travancore* and HMIS *Hindustan* to proceed to sea at 5 p.m. The former proceeded to the buoy, and waited for the latter to sail, as ordered. However, the ratings manning the *Hindustan* had other ideas. At 2.15 p.m. 11 ratings walked ashore without permission, shouting and gesticulating, followed by another five about two hours later. They were joined by 28 ratings from the *Travancore* and several others from the *Himalaya*, the Gunnery School. The ratings proceeded to the market at Keamari and urged the shop owners to down shutters. Shouting slogans such as 'Jai Hind' and 'Inquilab Zindabad' they marched in a procession to the Jackson Bazaar and the railway station, declaring that they were proceeding to Delhi. By 6 p.m., most of them returned to their ships but refused to go on board. Shortly afterwards, when the Captain of the *Hindustan* returned after meeting the Naval Officer-in-Charge, the ratings demanded the removal of the First Lieutenant for his insulting behaviour.

At about 7 a.m. on 21 February 1946, the ratings of the *Hindustan* were mustered. Four of them gave complaints to the Captain. At about 9 a.m., two of the men who had complaints accompanied the Captain to meet the Naval Officer-in-Charge, returning to the ship shortly afterwards. Meanwhile, about forty ratings of HMIS *Bahadur* proceeded to the quarter deck, pulled down and tore the Ensign, hoisting in its pace a 'Jai Hind' flag. They made their way to HMIS *Chamak*, the Radar Training School. However, when they tried to enter, the boys from *Chamak* resisted, but gave in after a while. The crowd then proceeded to HMIS *Himalaya*, which was similarly invaded. The Ensign was hauled down, window-panes broken, vehicles damaged and cells opened. The mob, which now had men from three ships—*Bahadur*, *Chamak* and *Himalaya*—then seized two landing craft and started moving towards Keamari from where they intended to go to Karachi.

When the two landing craft packed with ratings from Manora were about two hundred yards from the shore they were intercepted by two motor-boats carrying British parachutists. The Army captain in command ordered the landing craft to proceed towards China Creek but the ratings continued moving towards Keamari. At about 10 a.m. the landing craft with about 50 ratings, armed with hockey sticks and canes, came alongside the *Hindustan*. As the ratings were trying to board the *Hindustan* the parachutists from one of the boats opened fire. This was followed by firing from the quayside, which had been occupied by the military. The ratings of *Hindustan* loaded the Oerlikons and fired at the motor-boats, which moved towards China Creek. Some shots were also directed at a BOAC aircraft that was parked nearby. Two British soldiers were wounded, while two ratings from the *Bahadur* and three ratings from the *Himalaya*, who were in the crowd on board the *Hindustan*, died in the firing.

To prevent the ratings from marching intro the city as they had done on the previous day, the Army and Police had cordoned off the bridge connecting Keamari with Karachi. The ratings on board the *Hindustan* tried to break the cordon and enter the city but did not succeed. The enraged ratings gave an ultimatum that if the British troops were not withdrawn from the harbour they would open fire with the Oerlikons and other armament on board the ships. However, this did not have any effect and the Army pickets remained. During the night additional troops were moved into the harbour. Troops were deployed on the terrace of the buildings near the wharf and mounted artillery was positioned nearby.

At about 9 a.m. on 22 February 1946, Commodore Curtis went on board the *Hindustan* and asked the men to surrender, warning them that the Army action would begin at 9.30 if they did not surrender. At 10 a.m. another warning was issued giving a deadline of 10.30 a.m. for surrender. The ratings on the *Hindustan* responded by manning the ship's guns. They had decided not to give up without a fight. At 10.30 a.m. the British troops opened fire with 75 mm howitzers and mortars. The ratings retaliated with all armaments on board the ship, including the 4-inch guns. It was an unequal battle but the firing continued for about twenty minutes before the ratings gave up. At 10.50 a white flag was hoisted on the *Hindustan*, whose upper deck was on fire. Firing was stopped and the ratings surrendered to the Army. One rating each of *Hindustan*, *Travancore*, and *Chamak*, two of *Bahadur* and three of *Himalaya* were killed and several others wounded.[11]

Though the major events concerning the mutiny occurred at Bombay and Karachi, ships and establishments at other locations were also affected. HMIS *Kathiawar*, a minesweeper, was on a goodwill cruise along the Western Coast when the mutiny broke out at Bombay. The ship was at Porbander on 20 and 21 February when the ratings learned of the incidents at Bombay and Karachi on the wireless, with the officers remaining unaware of the mutiny. On 22 February the ship sailed for Veraval, its next port of call. However, without warning, the ratings seized control of the ship, confining all officers to the wardroom. The ship was turned around and set course for Karachi when information was received that the *Hindustan* had surrendered. The commanding officer resumed command but the ratings insisted that the goodwill cruise be called off and the ship should sail to Bombay, so that they could learn for themselves the true state of affairs.

By the time the ship reached Bombay on 23 February the strike had been called off.

The 37th Minesweeping Flotilla comprising the *Rohilkhand, Hongkong, Deccan, Bengal, Bihar, Baluchistan* and *Kistna*, was in the Andamans when the mutiny started in Bombay. The ships were anchored in Semaris Bay at Port Blair carrying out 'boiler cleaning', and were to resume minesweeping operations as soon as this was over. The ratings heard the news of the mutiny on BBC and All India Radio. They also received wireless messages asking them to join the strike. After the broadcast of Admiral Godfrey's message on 21 February tempers ran high and there was considerable unrest on all the ships. Next morning the ratings of the *Kistna* stopped work, and a motor-boat went around the harbour asking others to join the strike. In the evening a concert was arranged on the *Deccan*, which was attended by ratings from other ships also. The performance was interrupted by one of the ratings who announced that it was shameful that they were enjoying themselves while their brothers in Bombay were being killed. The concert was stopped and there was a lot of slogan shouting, which continued when the men returned to their ships. On 23 February the ratings of all the ships refused to fall in. They refused the orders of their officers and daily routine was not carried out. Though the mutiny was over the same evening, the men refused to resume work and insisted that the flotilla sail for Bombay. Commander Bailey, the senior officer present, visited all the ships and talked to the men but they were adamant. He had no choice and ordered the flotilla to sail for Bombay.

Commodore RP Khanna was serving on HMIS *Rohilkhand*, a minesweeper, as a sub-lieutenant when the mutiny took place. He was interviewed by the author on 11 September 2006 at his home in Vasant Vihar, New Delhi. According to him, the cause was not bad food, but ill-treatment by British officers, especially Captain King, the CO of Talwar, where the mutiny started. Most British officers who joined during the war were not from the right background. However, some like Commodore Knott and Commander Kilburn were very good. There was no national angle at that time. Later, political leaders such as Aruna Asaf Ali got involved. Sardar

Patel felt that their action was wrong and asked them to surrender. There was a strong anti-British feeling which was the root cause of the mutiny. Senior sailors told the CO and officers that they will not be harmed. When they reached Bombay, the Chief Bosun's mate escorted the officers to the Taj Mahal Hotel. There was no effect of the INA or any nationalist feelings among Indian officers. This was because there were very few Indian officers in the RIN at that time. There was large-scale demobilisation and many ships were de-commissioned. Most Indian officers felt that the mutiny was wrong. It had no support from Indian officers.[12]

The author also met Commodore Inder Singh who was posted as a lieutenant in a minesweeper, as the second-in-command, during the mutiny. During the interview, he said that the disaffection was due to maltreatment of Indian sailors by British officers of the RIN, which was called Really International Navy, due to the large number of nationalities from which officers were recruited—the UK, Russia, Norway, South Africa, etc. Most of them had been ratings and were promoted as officers during the war. They were arrogant and did not know how to handle Indians. They had no experience and knowledge about Indian religious sensibilities. Discrimination took many forms. Indian sailors in foreign ports were not allowed to buy items from NAAFI, like British sailors. Even Indian officers felt discriminated against. Indian food was not cooked in the Officers Mess. Some were diehards and very arrogant. The mutiny started on Talwar, where Commander King was this type of officer. His 2ic S.N. Kohli was on duty that day. King's predecessor was a very good officer who was fond of Indians. Inder Singh was sent by Admiral Rattray to Castle Barracks to talk to the men. Later, on 26 February he met Khan, the leader and asked him what his aim was? They had made their point and nothing would be gained by continuing the strike. He told him that the Barracks were surrounded by British troops and bombers were flying overhead. They could finish off the lot in a few minutes. Commander Katari and Lieutenant Commander Kohli met Nehru and asked him that as the political leader, he should tell them what to do. Nehru told them "thank you for telling me how to do my job" and dismissed them. There was no looting except for the luggage room in the Barracks being broken into, where baggage of officers was kept.[13]

HMIS *Valsura*, the Electrical and Torpedo Training School at Jamnagar, had about three hundred ratings. The ratings did not join the mutiny, but held a meeting on 21 February and passed some resolutions, which included a demand for the release of all sailors arrested at Bombay. On 23 February papers were found containing slogans such as 'Join the Talwar Strike', and 'Death to White Skins'. The same day some ratings from Bombay arrived with copies of the *Free Press Journal*, which had given wide coverage to the mutiny. After the mutiny ended at Bombay, a news broadcast on 24 February mentioned that the personnel of HMIS *Valsura* had not joined the strike. This agitated the ratings, who felt that it showed that they had no sympathy with their colleagues in Bombay. They decided to make amends and struck work on 25 February refusing to fall in. They surrendered on 26 February after a platoon of 26th Sikhs arrived to restore order.

At Calcutta, the ratings of the HMIS *Hooghly*, a shore establishment, refused duty on 19 February in sympathy with the men of the *Talwar*. The Commodore, Bay of Bengal spoke to the men who said that it was a peaceful strike. Next morning the sentries refused duty. The WRINs were sent away in view of the deteriorating situation. On 21 February the stewards, cooks and topasses at Lord Sinha road went on strike, instigated by the *Hooghly* men. The next two days passed off peacefully, but the strike continued. Finally, a military guard was posted on 24 February after which the strike ended.

In HMIS *India* at Delhi, some ratings in the Naval Barracks refused work on 20 February. The men were assembled but refused commands when called to attention on the arrival of the commanding officer. They were asked to nominate a representative who could put up their grievances. Finally, 56 men agreed to join duty while the rest refused. Next morning a platoon of Gurkhas arrived and placed 38 men under arrest.[14]

At Vizagapatnam, the naval units comprised the HMIS *Circars*, a shore establishment; three ships—HMISs *Sonavati*, *Ahmedabad* and *Shillong*— and certain flotillas. Effects of the mutiny in Bombay were felt only on

21 February. Ratings of the *Circars* hauled down the Ensign and shouted slogans in front of the Navy Office. They went to the golf course and shouted at the officers. The harbour signal centre hoisted a 'Jai Hind' flag. This was seen by the ratings of the *Sonavati* and *Shillong* who followed suit. Ratings from other ships boarded the *Ahmedabad* and asking the men to join them, pulled down the Ensign, which was promptly re-hoisted by the Quartermaster. Seventeen ratings left the ship to join the others. About half the ratings of the *Sonavati* also left. On 22 February, a conference was held in the Sub-Area Headquarters and the Army took over all naval establishments in Vizagapatnam. The mutineers were rounded up and taken in military custody. By 25 February all the ratings who had left their ships returned. The ringleaders were detained, with the rest being permitted to join their ships.[15]

Similar incidents occurred at several other stations. At Cochin the ratings of the HMIS *Baroda* struck work for 24 hours, while those of the HMIS *Venduruthy*, a shore establishment, remained unaffected. At Madras the ratings of the shore establishment HMIS *Adyar* decided to show their sympathy to the Bombay mutineers. Donning No. 10 dress they took out a procession and shouted slogans. An officer who asked them to go back was struck with a belt by a rating. However, they went back and joined duty. At the Wireless Telegraphy Station at Aden the ratings went on a hunger strike on 20 February when they heard about the strike at Bombay. The next day the three watches refused to carry out their duties, resulting in disruption in communications.[16]

The author met Commodore B.K. Dang at his house at D-4/8, Vasant Vihar, New Delhi on 15 December 2006. During the interview, he said:

> When the mutiny took place I was a sub-lieutenant at sea on ship INS *Tir*, in the Bay of Bengal. The CO was a British Jew called Joe Haakim, RNR. The 2ic was Lieutenant Sonpar. The British officers were eager to go back. Messages about the mutiny in Bombay were received by the signallers, who initially kept it from the officers. Sonpar came to know and confided in the Indian officers. The sailors locked up the CO in his cabin and pulled

down the ensign. I went down to the mess deck and talked to the men. I asked them 'what will you gain by revolting here at sea? Don't do anything until we reach Vizag'. The sailors agreed. The officers unlocked the CO's cabin and re-hoisted the ensign. They reached Vizag after two days. No formal enquiry was held. The incident was soft-pedalled by the officers. It did not spread because the officers were constantly in touch with the sailors.

The feeling was not widespread, the resentment being only against British officers. The mutiny did not start as a freedom movement. Politics entered only later. It was basically a food complaint that was badly handled by SN Kohli on INS *Talwar*. The provocative response by Kohli aggravated the situation. The underlying cause was frustration and uncertainty among the men due to demobilisation. Most of them were going to face an uncertain future and were therefore worried about resettlement.[17]

Several Boards of Inquiry were set up at the shore establishments and naval bases across India. The boards were instituted by the Naval authorities as fact-finding bodies to investigate the causes and circumstances of the mutiny. The boards consisted of British armed forces officers and primarily recorded testimonies of RIN officers with a small cross-section of ratings. The cause of the mutiny was determined to have its basis in administrative deficiencies such as inadequate information, failure of regular inspections, lack of experienced petty officers, chefs and officers.

On 8 March 1946, the Commander-in-Chief, General Claude Auchinleck recommended a Commission of Inquiry to determine the causes and origin of the mutiny. The Commission of Inquiry, constituted by the Government, was chaired by Sir S. Fazl Ali, Chief Justice of the Patna High Court. The two judicial members were Justice K.S. Krishnaswami Iyengar, Chief Justice of Cochin State, and Justice Mehr Chand Mahajan, of the Lahore High Court. The two service members were Vice Admiral W.R. Patterson, Flag Officer Commanding the Cruiser Squadron in East Indies Fleet, and Major General T.W. Rees, General Officer Commanding

4th Indian Division. The Commission began its deliberations in April and submitted its report in July 1946. The report of the Commission of Inquiry was publicly released in January 1947.

In its report, the Commission identified four main causes of the mutiny. These were discontent due to long-standing grievances; low state of morale, bad management and unsuitability of a large number of ratings; politics and the incidents that occurred on the *Talwar*. In its concluding remarks, the Commission commented:

> The basic cause of the mutiny in our opinion was widespread discontent among the Naval men arising mainly from a number of service grievances which had remained unredressed for some time and were aggravated by the political situation. Without this discontent, the mutiny would not have taken place.[18]

Though politics was listed as one of the causes of the mutiny, it was not among the major ones. It is true that the mutineers did approach several politicians, but their response was lukewarm. The first person they contacted was Aruna Asaf Ali, who was requested by the ratings of the *Talwar* to be their spokesman and take up their cause with national leaders. Not wishing to get involved in the strike, she advised them to remain calm and contact the "highest Congress authority in Bombay, Sardar Vallabhbhai Patel". When contacted by Aruna, Patel replied that since the ratings did not take his advice before resorting to the strike, he saw no reason why he or she should interfere. Patel's views were supported by the Bombay Provincial Congress Committee whose President, S. K. Patil, advised the ratings "to observe perfect discipline in their conduct and maintain an atmosphere of non-violence in all circumstances".[19]

Alarmed by the events that occurred on 21 and 22 February Aruna Asaf Ali wired Nehru, requesting him to come down to Bombay immediately to "control and avoid tragedy". Sardar Patel was equally perturbed by the violent turn of events, and wrote to the Governor of Bombay assuring him that the Congress Party would do its bit to control the violence and end the strike.

The leaders of the Muslim League, M.A. Jinnah and Liaquat Ali Khan, also felt it necessary to advise the mutineers to call off the strike. The issue was discussed in the Central Legislative Assembly on 22 and 23 February 1946. On 26 February 1946 Nehru and Patel addressed a gathering at Chowpatty in Bombay, decrying the violence, while commending the ratings for their patriotic spirit. The only leader who came out unequivocally against the mutiny was Mahatma Gandhi. Unlike most other political leaders who preferred to call it a strike, Gandhi was very clear that it was a mutiny. In a statement to the Press on 23 February 1946 at Poona he said:

> I have followed the events now happening in India with painful interest. This mutiny in the navy and what is following is not, in any sense of the term, non-violent action… Destruction of churches and the like is not the way to swaraj as defined by the Congress. Burning of tramcars and other property, insulting and injuring Europeans is not non-violence of the Congress type, much less mine, if and in so far as it may be different from the Congress. Let the known and unknown leaders of this thoughtless orgy of violence know what they are doing and then follow their bend. Let it not be said that India of the Congress spoke to the world of winning swaraj through non-violent action and belied her word in action and that too at the critical period in her life. … If the Indian members of the Navy know and appreciate non-violence, the way of non-violent resistance can be dignified, manly and wholly effective, if it is corporate. For the individual it always is. Why should they continue to serve, if service is humiliating for them or India? … As it is, they are setting a bad and unbecoming example for India.[20]

Though not inspired by political reasons, the RIN mutiny did have political consequences. It was preceded by the RIAF mutiny and followed by several mutinies in the Army, including one at the Signal Training Centre at Jubbulpore. Together, these caused consternation and alarm in Delhi and London. The realisation that Britain could no longer depend on the Indian Armed Forces was partly responsible for her decision to quit

India in 1947. Recognising this contribution, the Government of India subsequently agreed to accord the ratings who participated in the mutiny the status of freedom fighters. In June 1973 the Government approved the grant of freedom fighters' pension to 476 personnel who had lost their jobs, being dismissed or discharged from service because of their role in the mutiny.[21]

Notes
1. Report of the Commission of Inquiry—RIN Mutiny 1946, Ministry of Defence, History Division (MODHD), New Delhi, Document 601/7968/1, pp. 20-27.
2. Rear Admiral Satyindra Singh, *Under Two Ensigns—The Indian Navy 1945-1950* (New Delhi, 1986), p. 55.
3. Dilip Kumar Das, *Revisiting Talwar—A Study in the Royal Indian Navy Uprising of February 1946* (New Delhi, 1993), p. 63.
4. Das, p. 74.
5. Das, pp. 77-78.
6. Report of the Commission of Inquiry, p. 53.
7. Das, p. 164.
8. Report of the Commission of Inquiry, p. 56.
9. *The Free Press Journal*, Bombay, 22 February 1946.
10. Report of the Commission of Inquiry, p. 59.
11. Report of the Commission of Inquiry, p. 100.
12. Commodore R. P. Khanna, interview with author, 11 September 2006.
13. Author's interview with Commodore Inder Singh at his house at 12 Poorvi Marg, Vasant Vihar, New Delhi on 20 December 2006.
14. Report of the Commission of Inquiry, pp. 106-107.
15. Report of the Commission of Inquiry, pp. 109-112.
16. Report of the Commission of Inquiry, p. 113.
17. Commodore BK Dang, interview with author, 15 December 2006.
18. Report of the Commission of Inquiry, p. 498.
19. *The Free Press Journal*, Bombay, 22 February 1946.
20. Mahatma Gandhi, *Collected Works*, vol. 89, p. 441.
21. Satyindra Singh, p. 90.

3
The Air Force Mutiny—1946

The mutiny in the RIAF (Royal Indian Air Force) occurred at almost the same time as the more serious uprisings in the RIN (Royal Indian Navy) and Army Signals Centre at Jubbulpore in February 1946. Some historians prefer to call it a strike rather than a mutiny, since there was no violence and neither was anyone punished. However, the term 'strike' is usually not used in the armed forces, collective disobedience always being called a mutiny, irrespective of the number of persons involved and the gravity of the insubordination. Though they occurred at almost the same time, the trouble in the RIAF was quite different from the uprisings that occurred in the other two services. While the disturbances in the Army and the RIN were confined to Indian soldiers and sailors, the unrest in the RIAF was induced by 'strikes' by British airmen of the RAF (Royal Air Force). Since no disciplinary action was taken against the British airmen, the authorities had to take a lenient view of the indiscipline by Indian airmen also. Unlike the uprisings in the Navy and the Army that had some nationalistic element, the demands of the RIAF personnel related mostly to pay, rations and travel concessions.

Though the RIAF mutiny was controlled without the use of force, it had far-reaching implications. The Indian Air Force—the prefix Royal was added only in 1943—was just six years old when World War II began, undergoing a tenfold increase in size by the time it ended. Though still minuscule compared to the Indian Army, it was a potent force that could no longer be ignored. Coupled with the more serious incidents in the other two armed forces, it reinforced the perception of the British authorities that the Indian troops could no longer be relied upon to maintain Britain's hold over India. This necessitated a serious review of British policy, leading ultimately to the decision to pull out of India.

Three Indians pilots held commissions in the RAF during World War I, fighting with great gallantry. They were Lieutenant H.S. Malik, 2nd Lieutenant E.S.C. Sen and Lieutenant Indra Lal Roy. Sen was shot down over Germany and became a prisoner of war, while Roy was killed in air combat in July 1918. It was only in 1930 that a decision was taken to establish an air force in India. Officers selected as pilots were sent to Cranwell in UK for training, while the ground staff, recruited as *hawai sepoys* (air soldiers) were trained in India. The first batch of five Indians commissioned as pilot officers comprised Sircar, Subroto Mukerjee, Bhupinder Singh, A. Singh and A.D. Dewan. The IAF (Indian Air Force) formally came into being on 1 April 1933, when the first Indianised squadron—No. 1 Squadron—was formed at Karachi, exactly 15 years after the creation of the RAF.[1]

Shortly after the outbreak of World War II, it was decided to form the IAFVR (Indian Air Force Volunteer Reserve) to take over the task of coastal defence from the RAF. Following the commencement of the Japanese offensive in South East Asia in December 1941, a flight of the IAFVR was flown to Moulmein to carry out anti-submarine and convoy protection operations. After the capture of Moulmein by Japanese forces, No. 3 IAFVR Squadron was sent to Rangoon for reconnaissance and convoy protection duties. As British forces withdrew in the face of the relentless Japanese offensive, No. 1 Squadron arrived at Toungoo, where they were subjected to raids by the Japanese Air Force on the first day itself. During the next two days, Squadron Leader K.K. 'Jumbo' Majumdar led the whole squadron on raids against the Japanese base at Mehingson inflicting severe damage and earning a great moral victory. The exploit not only made Majumdar a hero overnight but also enhanced the reputation of the fledgling IAF in its first major operation during the war. In view of its splendid performance during the war, the IAF was given the prefix 'Royal' on its tenth anniversary, becoming the RIAF (Royal Indian Air Force) on 1 April 1943.

From one squadron in 1939 the IAF had grown to three by the beginning of 1942, the year which saw the greatest expansion in its size. By the end of 1942, it had seven squadrons; during the next year another two were added, bringing its strength to nine squadrons by the beginning of 1944. The number of personnel had increased correspondingly, from 16 officers and 269 airmen at the beginning of the war to 1,200 officers and over 20,000 trained airmen, with another 6,000 undergoing training, besides about 2,000 followers. In the early years of the war, 20 Indian pilots had been sent to the UK to help the RAF, which had run perilously short of pilots during the Battle of Britain. These Indian pilots served in RAF squadrons and did sterling work during the critical months, carrying out fighter sweeps over France and escorting bombers. Seven Indian pilots were killed in operations, the remainder returning to India in mid-1942. One of the pilots who returned from the German front with a DFC was K.K. Majumdar, who later died in an air crash at Lahore in February 1945.[2]

While World War I lasted four years, World War II continued for six years. When it ended in 1945, everyone was weary and drained out. Many of the participants had been away from their homes for several years and were eagerly looking forward to a reunion with their families. Demobilisation began soon after the end of the war, but the sheer numbers of servicemen, especially from the USA and UK, made the process slow and time-consuming. Hundreds of thousands of troops were literally doing nothing, waiting for ships to take them home from remote and inhospitable corners of the globe. The wait seemed interminable, and most men were unable to comprehend the reasons for the delay in sending them home. Coupled with the delay in repatriation, another major problem was the uncertain future that most of the men faced. Resettlement and rehabilitation measures obviously could not cater for all the servicemen, who knew that they would have to fend for themselves. Wartime industries that employed millions of workers were closing down, and most of the men shedding uniforms had neither the training nor the experience for the new enterprises that were coming up.

The first sign of unrest came from American troops based in Germany who held mass parades to demand speedier demobilisation and repatriation. These parades were given wide publicity on the American forces programmes that were very popular and eagerly heard by servicemen all over the world. Similar demonstrations by American soldiers in Calcutta could not leave British troops serving in South East Asia unaffected and it was only a matter of time before the virus spread to other stations. Apart from the logistics, another reason for the slow rate of demobilisation of British servicemen was the uncertainty about the future of British rule in India. As late as June 1946, the Chiefs of Staff in London were still considering various options, one of which was to continue British rule in India, for which seven additional divisions would be needed. This would naturally result in suspending the process of demobilisation, with serious implications, especially the effect on morale.[3]

Taking a cue from the Americans, British airmen at the RAF base at Mauripur refused to join duty on 22 January 1946. The Inspector General of the RAF, Air Chief Marshal Sir Arthur Barratt, who was on tour in South East Asia, and was passing through Mauripur at the time, held a meeting with the men to ascertain their grievances. The men had many complaints, most of which were related to aspects of demobilisation that could only be dealt with at a higher level by the Cabinet or the Air Ministry. One such grievance was, "Why is RAF demobilisation so slow compared with that in the Army and the Navy?" Air Chief Marshal Barratt explained that practically all the points raised by the men had been explained in the demobilisation forms which were a part of the release scheme and kept the personnel fully in the picture, explaining the reasons for the various actions taken, especially with regard to the release under classes 'B' and 'C'.

The men were not satisfied and demanded that a Parliamentary representative should visit them so that they could impress upon him, and he on Parliament, their feelings about the slow speed of demobilisation. A Parliamentary delegation was then in India and they asked that it should visit Mauripur. Air Chief Marshal Barratt assured the men that he would forward their demands to Air Ministry, and asked the men to return to work but they refused. He warned the airmen that nothing would be obtained under threat and urged them to return to duty. The meeting ended with no promises made. The Air Officer Commanding 229 Group stated that he would be able to get the men back to work that afternoon. After making his report to the Air Ministry, the Inspector General proceeded on his prearranged tour programme. The situation remained unchanged in the evening. Many of the men showed an inclination to join duty but appeared to be fearful of rough treatment at the hands of others.

In his report to the Air Ministry, Air Chief Marshal Barratt had mentioned all their grievances, asking for a reply to be sent to the Air Officer Commanding India. As regards the demand for the Parliamentary delegation already in India to visit Mauripur, he felt that the delegation was visiting parts of the Commonwealth for an entirely different purpose and it would not be wise to permit the members to address the men, as they were not well-versed in the intricacies of the demobilisation policy of the government and did not understand the feelings of the personnel in South East Asia. However, it was possible for Mr. Harold Davies, the MP for Leek, who was visiting South East Asia, to meet the airmen. Mr. Davies had already visited units in India, Burma and Malaya in order to keep the men in touch with the new Government's policy and, during his tour, had spoken to hundreds of servicemen.[4]

News of the strike at Mauripur soon spread to Ceylon, the first unit being affected being at Negombo, where the personnel of No. 32 Staging Post refused to carry out servicing of aircraft. The morning York service from Mauripur on 23 January 1946 was serviced by the aircrew themselves, giving an indication that something was amiss. As at Mauripur, the major complaint was that of slow demobilisation, the other grievances being bad administration and lack of sports facilities and entertainment. The men felt that personnel of the Fleet Air Arm should be drafted into the RAF to assist with key trades, and expedite the RAF release. Another cause for complaint was that RAF airmen were being asked to work on BOAC and Qantas aircraft. The men felt that this had two effects: firstly, that the air passage of civilians was delaying release of servicemen, and secondly, that the employment of airmen was providing aviation companies with cheap labour.

The Air Officer Commanding, Air Commodore Chilton was on his way to the Cocos Islands when he received news of the strike. He returned to Negombo and talked to the men, promising to remedy the local problems straightaway. As regards the drafting of personnel of the Fleet Air Arm, speeding up demobilisation and servicing of civilian aircraft, he assured them that these would be forwarded to the Air Ministry. With the resolution of grievances concerning administration, sports facilities and entertainment, it was hoped that the men would resume duty on the following day. Air Commodore Chilton decided to continue his flight since the news of the Negombo incident had reached 129 Staging Post in the Cocos Islands where it was understood that the airmen intended taking similar action.

However, on his arrival at the Cocos Islands, he found the station running smoothly, with no sign of trouble. While he was visiting the station, he received a signal asking him to return to Negombo where the situation had deteriorated. The stoppage of work by the airmen had spread from the Staging Post to the rest of the station, including the Communication and Meteorological Flights. The men were well behaved but adamant. The Air Officer Commanding tried to convince the men that no good would come of their strike irrespective of what was happening in India. The men continued to complain of the delays regarding repatriation and mails. It was pointed out that by refusing to work they would delay their release and mails even more. Releases were governed by the Manpower Committee in London and the local RAF authorities could do little more than forward the complaints to the Air Ministry.

By this time the disaffection had spread and by 26 January airmen at Koggala, Ratmalana and Colombo were also involved. It was apparent from reports received from various units that broadcasts made by the BBC on 24 and 25 January were largely responsible for the information reaching them, bringing out feelings that were dormant and encouraging them to emulate their colleagues who had joined the strike. Except at Negombo where the relations between the Station and Staging Post were not easy, at other stations the unit commanders and officers were in close touch with the men, addressing them at the first sign of trouble. However, the problems concerning repatriation and release could not be solved by them on their own, though every effort was made to take the men into confidence and explain the policy in this regard. Many of the grievances, such as disparity in releases compared to RAF personnel in UK and faster repatriation of personnel of the Navy and Army were unfounded.

Meanwhile, the strikes in RAF stations in India continued to spread. On 26 January 1946, Air Marshal Sir Roderick Carr, Air Officer Commanding, British Air Forces in South East Asia, sent a signal to the Air Ministry giving details of the stoppage of work that had occurred at Palam, Dum Dum, Poona, Cawnpore and Vizagapatnam, in addition to Mauripur. Except at Mauripur, all stoppages were of short duration but it was considered that other units were likely to be affected. The majority of units were 'striking' in an orderly and respectful manner in order to register a protest against the Government's policy, and then returning to work. Air Marshal Carr considered that unless the Government shouldered the responsibility of making a comprehensive statement, even if that statement did not meet the airmen's requirements, he anticipated that the men would strike again. Units that had returned to work had done so on the assumption that their dissatisfaction with the demobilisation policy had been presented to the Government from which they were expecting a comprehensive statement. No promises were made, but the men had been informed that the questions raised in the Inspector General's report had been forwarded to the Secretary of State. In conclusion, Air Marshal Carr stressed that he saw no alternative to a Government statement. While he agreed that the Government should not be called upon to issue a general statement as a concession to indiscipline, he felt that in this instance, failure to do so it may have serious consequences.

The stoppage of work on RAF stations in India influenced the personnel of the RIAF also. Reports of men staying away from work were received from Trichinopoly and No. 228 Group. The main cause of discontent—demobilisation—was augmented by complaints regarding leave, food and family allowances. In addition to speeding up their release, the Indian airmen requested that family and ration allowances should be paid to them while on leave. They maintained that granting only one free rail warrant per annum meant hardship to airmen who had to split their leave in two or three parts. They requested that either additional railway warrants should be given or permission granted to avail their entire leave at one time during the year.

The strikes in the RIAF alarmed the authorities, since they could have an adverse effect on the political situation in the country. The Air Marshal Commanding, British Air Forces in South East Asia sent a signal to all RAF units informing them of this. The signal, which was not sent to RIAF units, read:

> The Government plan for demobilization must be a balanced one: our industries at home require manpower, but this cannot be provided at the risk of endangering the safety of the World. There are still defence problems in India. The public press has recently made it clear that a political crisis is approaching, a crisis which may only be solved by little short of civil war. If you wish, you may quote me as authority for this. The Government at Home are now fully aware that conscripts in the RAF have little or no pride in their service. I do not believe that these misguided airmen who took part in the recent so-called strikes appreciate that their action may be endangering the safety of India. Already their example has been followed by the RIAF. Such actions can only encourage civil disturbances and may lead to grave consequences for everyone in India including those airmen who are not due for repatriation in the near future.[5]

The Allied Air Commander-in-Chief, Air Chief Marshal Sir Keith Park was also concerned by the RIAF strikes. He signalled all commanders in South East Asia, stressing that it was essential that pay and allowances and other conditions of service in the post-war Indian Air Force should be made known to all concerned, with the least possible delay. The Government of India had set up a committee to examine and make recommendations on the terms and conditions of service to be applied to the post-war Indian forces, including the Air Force. The work of the committee would be hastened with due regard to the necessity of arriving at a well-considered conclusion. The message continued:

> I have collected from various sources a full list of the grievances of the Royal Indian Air Force airmen and will do everything in my power to have them investigated. To do this thoroughly will take time. I must make it clear to all concerned that I cannot condone the serious breaches of discipline that have taken place during the last twelve days, and any improvement in conditions that I may be able to make will not, repeat, not be a concession to discipline. I will always accept honest complaints if passed to me through the correct channels. I would like to assure both officers and other ranks personnel who desire to continue in the service that the Royal Indian Air Force offers a fine career to the right man.

Meanwhile, the strikes in RAF stations continued to spread, with the most serious incident occurring at Seletar in Singapore on 26 January 1946, followed by a similar incident at Kallang on the very next day. The Allied Air Commander-in-Chief visited Seletar and had detailed discussions with the men, which he reported to the Air Ministry. Realising the seriousness of the matter, the British Prime Minister, Mr. Clement Attlee, made a statement in the House of Commons on 29 January outlining the measures being taken to expedite repatriation and release, which seemed to be the root cause of the trouble. On the same day the men of 194 (Transport) Squadron in Rangoon stopped work. However, they returned to work the next day. The unit was scheduled for disbandment in the near future but in view of this incident, it was disbanded on 15 February 1946.

The mutiny by ratings of the Royal Indian Navy in February 1946 added a new dimension to the problem, especially at Bombay, where the RIAF airmen went on a sympathetic strike. To subdue the mutineers who had taken control of ships and were threatening to bombard Bombay, one of the measures being seriously considered was air attacks using rocket projectiles. However, in view of the strike by RIAF personnel, the authorities felt that Indian squadrons could not be used for this purpose. Responding to an appeal from Sir Roderick Carr, Air Officer Commanding British Air Forces in South East Asia, the Allied Air Commander-in-Chief, Sir Keith Park agreed to divert some aircraft from his resources. However, in view of the recent experience in Java, he advised Carr to obtain the approval of the C-in-C India before using RAF and RIAF aircraft in an offensive role against the local population.[6]

RIAF personnel refused to report for duty at many stations for varying periods. The Naval strike came to an end on 23 February 1946, leading to improvement in the situation at Bombay, though the airmen had still not resumed duty. Other than Bombay, the stations that continued to be affected were Cawnpore, Allahabad and Jodhpur, though conditions seemed to be improving and were expected to become normal soon. However, a serious incident occurred in Rangoon, where 140 RIAF personnel failed to report for duty on 23 February. When asked for their grievances, the airmen listed the following demands:

- Equal rights with BORs in the Unit canteen.
- Equal distribution of Unit dues between the RAF and RIAF.
- Separate Mess for RIAF with half BOR and half Indian type rations.
- Weekly show of Indian films.
- Separate recreation room with Indian periodicals.
- Full entitlement of leave for all RIAF personnel.
- Better living conditions.
- Higher scale of pay and allowances.
- Second class railway warrants.
- Speed up demobilisation.

On the night of 24 February the Commanding Officer interviewed two of the men's representatives and informed them that their grievances had been forwarded to the Air Marshal Commanding Air Headquarters

Burma. Grievances that could be resolved locally would be dealt by the Air Marshal personally while the remaining questions concerning pay, allowances and demobilisation would be forwarded to higher authorities. The Commanding Officer emphasised that the men must return to duty before their demands could be considered. The representatives agreed and gave an assurance that they would do so, but the men did not join duty until 28 February 1946.

In February there was a strike at Kohat, the only Air Force station in India manned by the RIAF, where the Station Commander was Group Captain (later Air Chief Marshal) A.M. 'Aspy' Engineer. An account of the strike and how it was handled has been described by Squadron Leader (later Air Vice Marshal) Harjinder Singh, who was then posted at Air Force Station Peshawar. On 26 February, Harjinder received a telephone call from Flight Lieutenant Shahzada, Adjutant of the Air Force Station Kohat informing him that the airmen had gone on strike that morning. The men had collected at the aerodrome from where they intended to take out a protest march through the city. Group Captain Engineer had asked the Adjutant to inform Harjinder that he had already requisitioned some Gurkha troops from the Army to erect a roadblock at the aerodrome gate, and if necessary, open fire on the strikers if they tried to force their way out. Harjinder asked his Station Commander, Group Captain Vallaine, to permit him to fly to Kohat, without giving him any reason. Fortunately, Vallaine agreed, and detailed Flying Officer Glandstein to take Harjinder to Kohat in a Harvard aircraft.

After reaching Kohat, Harjinder reported to the Station Commander who gave him some more details of the strike. Apparently, the men were in no mood to listen to any officer and he advised Harjinder not to go near them. Harjinder felt that unless the situation was brought under control immediately, it would be the end of the only Indian Air Force station in the country. He asked for permission to approach the strikers and talk to them. Engineer refused, but when Harjinder insisted, he relented, telling the latter that that he would not be responsible for his life. When Harjinder approached the strikers, who had collected on the airstrip, one of them shouted: "Don't let this officer come near, because he will call off the strike." But there were others who differed, and wanted him to come. Harjinder proposed that they take a vote by show of hands, and was pleasantly surprised when the majority elected to hear him. After talking to the men, Harjinder found that they had heard that it was planned to bomb and machine gun the Naval ratings who had gone on strike in Bombay. When asked for their demands, they said that the Station Commander should send a message to the Commander-in-Chief in Delhi telling him that the Indian Air Force Station Kohat refuses to cooperate in bombing their colleagues in the Navy. Also, in the signal it should be clearly mentioned that the Air Force Station Kohat sympathises with the relatives of the people who have been killed in the firing at Bombay. The rest of the story is best described by Harjinder in his own words:

> To my mind, it was a reasonable demand and I asked them: "Is that all?" and they all said "Yes". So, I told them: "I will guarantee that the Station Commander will do what you have asked, and what is more, there was never an intention of sending Indian Air Force Squadrons to bomb and machine-gun our naval colleagues and there must have been some misunderstanding."
>
> After addressing the men further and quietening them down I told them that they had disgraced themselves by striking, and before it was too late they should report back to work; and as a first consequence, they should immediately fall in. The men readily agreed. I got them fallen-in in three ranks and marched them to the Cinema hall. I told them to accept any punishment that the Station Commander gave without hesitation and if the station Commander asked them: "Did you go on strike?" they should say "No, we never had any such intention." It took me exactly ten minutes to settle the issue in this way.
>
> After marching the airmen into the Cinema hall, I reported to the Station Commander and briefed him on what to say. In fairness to Aspy I must

say he sent the signal to General Auchinleck on the lines that I had promised the airmen. When he went into the Cinema hall and asked the men whether they had intended to go on strike, the men with one voice shouted: "No." As planned, he said: "All right, but as a punishment for your indiscipline this morning, I am ordering extra parades in the afternoon for the whole Station for one month." They filed out of the hall quietly enough.

After the 'strike' was over, I took off for Peshawar. Some days later I heard that the Station Commander had been called up by Delhi and given a sound dressing down because of the signal which he had sent concerning the Indian Naval mutiny at Bombay.[7]

Another strike that was defused by an Indian officer was the one at the Factory Road Camp in Delhi. The strike lasted four days and was eventually broken by sympathetic handling by Group Captain (later Air Chief Marshal) Subroto Mukerjee, who was ably assisted by Warrant Officer Verghese. After the strike ended, RAF Intelligence was asked to identify the ringleaders. Based on their report, Air Headquarters decided to discharge the personnel involved in the strike. Surprisingly, the first name on the list was that of Warrant Officer Verghese, who had been instrumental in subduing the strike. It was only after Subroto Mukerjee intervened with Air Marshal Sir Rodrick Carr that the orders for Verghese's discharge were withdrawn.

During the course of his research, the author met Marshal of the Air Force Arjan Singh at his residence at 7A Kautilya Marg, Chanakyapuri, New Delhi on 11 September 2006. During the interview, the MAF talked not only about the RIAF mutiny but also his experiences during the battle of Imphal where he was posted with No. 1 Squadron in 1943-1944. He said that they knew that Japan wanted to take India. Bose was made much of by Bengalis. However, the INA was not held in high regard. Burhanuddin (who later joined the INA) was one of the six officers attached to the RIAF in 1940 to make up the deficiency of Air Force officers. They had no flying experience and none did well. The experiment was not repeated. He had no respect for people who were captured in Singapore. They made no attempt to escape. At least the INA did something for independence though they were misguided and did not know the real intentions of the Japs. As regards the RIAF Mutiny, he said that anti-British feeling was there because the troops were more educated. The British decided to leave due to disaffection in the Armed Forces. There was good rapport between Indian and British officers.[8]

Though officially classified as a mutiny, the incidents in the RIAF were actually nothing more than 'strikes'. In almost all cases, the airmen resorted to stoppage of work or a sit-down strike. There was no slogan shouting, waving of flags or processions, as happened in the mutinies in the other two services that occurred at almost the same time. There was no violence or use of force, and in most cases the strikes ended after the intervention of officers who assured the men that their grievances would be looked into sympathetically. None of the participants were punished, though a few of the ringleaders were discharged from service. Though the strikes were not serious, they brought to light the feeling of discontent among the Indian personnel serving in the Air Force, forcing the British authorities to review the dependability of the armed forces in India. This played a part in the decision of the British to quit India in 1947.

Notes

1. Air Commodore A.L. Saigal (ed.), *Birth of an Air Force—The Memoirs of Air Vice Marshal Harjinder Singh* (New Delhi, 1977), p. 34.
2. Air Commodore A.L. Saigal (ed.), *Birth of an Air Force—The Memoirs of Air Vice Marshal Harjinder Singh* (New Delhi, 1977), p. 216.
3. Nicholas Mansergh and Penderel Moon (eds.) *The Transfer of Power 1942-47*, 12 vols. (London, 1982), vol. vii, pp. 889-900.
4. *A Brief History of Events Associated with the Disaffection and 'Strikes' Among Personnel in the RAF Units of Air Command, South East Asia*, Ministry of Defence, History Division (MODHD), New Delhi, 601/9768/H, pp. 1-2.
5. *A Brief History of Events Associated with the Disaffection and 'Strikes' Among Personnel in the RAF Units of Air Command, South East Asia*, Ministry of Defence, History Division (MODHD), New Delhi, 601/9768/H, p. 10.

6. *A Brief History of Events Associated with the Disaffection and 'Strikes' Among Personnel in the RAF Units of Air Command, South East Asia*, Ministry of Defence, History Division (MODHD), New Delhi, 601/9768/H, p. 24.
7. Air Commodore A.L. Saigal (ed.), *Birth of an Air Force—The Memoirs of Air Vice Marshal Harjinder Singh* (New Delhi, 1977), pp. 218-21.
8. Marshal of the Air Force Arjan Singh, interview with author, 11 September 2006.

4
Brief History of The Corps of Signals

Brief History

The Corps of Signals, or the Indian Signal Corps as it was known before Independence, did not come into being in one clearly defined step. It went through several stages of development, till it attained its present form. In a sense, the Corps was not born, but came into being through a natural process of evolution. In the first phase, prior to 1911, signalling arrangements were ad hoc, without any fixed organisation responsible for this task. The second phase, from 1911 to 1920, saw the creation of the Signal Service as a separate entity, in the form of signal companies of the Sappers and Miners. The third phase commenced in 1920 with the formation of the Indian Signal Corps, and lasted till 1947, when India achieved freedom from British rule and became an independent nation. The fourth phase covers the growth of the Corps of Signals in the post-Independence Indian Army. Only the period prior to 1946 is covered in this chapter.

There is no authentic record of any army communications in India before 1857, when the electric telegraph was used effectively for conveying information regarding the uprising, and facilitating its suppression. Captain P. Stewart, who had replaced O'Shaughnessy as Superintendent of the Electric Telegraph, laid a line from Cawnpore (now Kanpur) to Lucknow in record time, during the relief operations led by the Commander-in-Chief, Sir Colin Campbell. This elicited an eloquent tribute from the correspondent of the *London Times*, who wrote,

> "Never since its discovery, has the electric telegraph played so important and daring a role as it does now in India. Without it the commander-in-

chief would lose the effect of half his forces. It has served him better than his right arm."¹

Up to the end of the 19th century, there were three armies in India, belonging to the Presidencies of Bengal, Bombay and Madras. Each had its own Corps of Sappers and Miners, which were responsible for signalling, in addition to their basic tasks. Field telegraphy was a jealously guarded preserve of the Indian Telegraph Department (ITD), and Army Signalling was a military skill, exercised by British officers and soldiers making use of flags, lamps and heliograph. In 1890, the ITD was made responsible for communications up to Force Headquarters, with the assistance of instructional squads provided by the Sappers and Miners. Forward communications were provided by regimental signallers, who were taken from units in accordance with the needs of the operation or expedition. This was the arrangement followed for the campaigns in Burma (1885-1887), Waziristan (1894-1895), Chitral (1895), the Tochi Field Force (1897), Mallakand (1897), Mohmand Field Force (1897), and Tibet (1903-1904).

Lord Kitchener, the Commander-in-Chief, India, having reorganised the Cavalry and Infantry, turned to Signals and proposed the formation of four telegraph companies, each of 120 men. The proposals were approved in 1908, but never implemented. In 1909, a committee was set up in England to coordinate methods of communication, and based on its report, a similar committee was formed in India, which recommended the raising of four divisional signal companies and a wireless section. The Viceroy accepted the proposals, and forwarded them to London on 4 August 1910, requesting sanction of the Secretary of State for India 'by telegram'. The Secretary of State for India responded with commendable alacrity and economy on 21 September: *"Your confidential despatch 87, dated 4th August last. Signal companies. I sanction scheme."*²

In October 1910, Lieut. Colonel S.H. Powell, R.E. was posted to Army Headquarters to organise a Signal Service for India. Though his designation was GSO 1 in the Staff Duties Directorate, Powell in effect became the first head of the Indian Signal Service, which later became the Indian Signal

Corps. By November 1910, the schedule of raising of the four divisional signal companies and the wireless company had been finalised. Companies 31and 32 were raised on 15 February 1911 at Fatehgarh, followed by 33 and 34 Companies and the nucleus of 41 Wireless Company on 1 March at Roorkee. The Commandants of the companies were: Captain H.S.E. Franklin, 15 Ludhiana Sikhs (31 Company); Captain W.F. Maxwell, R.E., 3rd Sappers & Miners (32 Company); Captain L.H. Queripel, Royal Field Artillery (33 Company); Captain R.G. Earle, R.E., 2nd Queen Victoria's Own Sappers & Miners (34 Company); and Captain D.A. Thompson, R.E., 1st King George's Own Sappers & Miners (41 Wireless Company).

The organisation of the signal companies was issued as a Special Army Order dated 3 February 1911.The companies were to be Sappers and Miners units, and their sepoys were to rank as sappers. However, each company was to be a corps for the purposes of enrolment, enlistment and discharge of Indian personnel. Apart from the Commandant, there were four British officers (subalterns) and 44 British other ranks (BOR) in each company. The Indian personnel comprised two Indian officers (later known as VCOs), 86 other ranks, and 11 followers. Six horses were authorised for British mounted signallers and two ponies for Indian linemen. British officers of all arms and services were seconded to the signal companies for four years. British other ranks could be transferred from British and Indian units of the Indian Army. Indian personnel could be recruited directly by the Commandants or Recruiting Officers. The class composition of 31 and 32 Companies, which were allotted to Northern Command, was half Mussalmans from Punjab or United Provinces and half Dogras and Rajputs. Companies 33 and 34, allotted to Southern Command, had half Madrassi Mussalmans and half Tamils, Christians and Pariahs.

Signals in the British Army were reorganised almost at the same time as in the Indian Army. Telegraph companies of the Royal Engineers were responsible for all forms of signalling till 1910 when the term 'telegraph' was replaced by 'signal' in unit titles. In 1912, motorcyclists were added to their establishment, for operating the signal despatch service. With this, the Signal Service became responsible for all types of signalling in the British Army, including electric telegraph, telephone, visual signalling, wireless and signal despatch. This organisation was similar to what obtained in the Indian Army, when World War I broke out in 1914. During the War, the signal organisation was found to be wanting, especially with regard to tactical communications for the artillery, administrative installations, amphibious operations and cooperation with the air arm. The absence of a Director of Signals at Army Headquarters and signal staff at subordinate levels was felt in Britain as well as in India. The shortfall in resources can be gauged from the fact that, in India, ten additional signal companies had to be raised between 1916 and 1918, beside several Line of Communication signal units for Mesopotamia and East Africa. The total strength of Signals went up from 604 in 1914 to 10,243 at the end of the War.

The proposal to create a separate Signal Corps to replace the Signal Service was initiated by the War Office in London in September 1918, even before the end of World War I. After considerable discussion and deliberation, the proposal was accepted, and a Royal Warrant was issued on 28 June 1920, conveying the approval for the formation of the Corps of Signals as a separate entity in the British Army. On 5 August the King conferred on the new corps the title of 'Royal'. In India, similar changes took place after the War. On 17 April 1920, an Army Department Notification ruled that all signal units (of the Sappers and Miners) would be included as a corps in the Indian Army Act Rules, with the designation Indian Signal Corps. For some reason, the staff overlooked this, and signal units continued to be shown in the Indian Army List as the Indian Signal Service, Sappers and Miners. It became necessary to issue another Indian Army Order on 12 November 1922, which drew attention to the Indian Army Act Rules and specified that the new designation should be used in future. Interestingly, the Corps of Signals in India considers 15 February 1911, when the first divisional signal companies were raised, as the date of its birth, which makes it nine years older than the Royal Signals!

Changes also took place in the signal staff at various levels. Two new commands had been created in November 1920, taking their number to four. An Assistant Director of Signals was appointed at each command headquarters. This designation was changed to Chief Signal Officer in June 1921, and has remained unchanged till today. At Army Headquarters, the appointment of Inspector of Signals was abolished on 1 January 1919 and an Assistant Director of Army Signals appointed in his place. This designation was changed to Chief Signal Officer in June 1920, and a year later, to Signal Officer-in-Chief. This appointment still exists, both in the British and the Indian armies.

Minor changes in signal organisation continued, though the basic structure remained unchanged till the outbreak of World War II. In November 1920, numbers were replaced by alphabets in unit titles, and divisional signal companies were redesignated as divisional signals. In 1923, the number of classes was reduced to five, and in 1925 to only four—Punjabi Mussalmans, Dogras, Sikhs, and Mixed Madrassis. In 1926, the system of relief of signal units was discontinued, and only personnel were relieved individually. In 1927, three of the seven divisional signals were redesignated as district signals, while the remaining were given numbers from 01 to 04. Several measures were initiated towards gradual Indianisation of Corps. In 1928, British other ranks were removed from line construction and cable sections. In 1934, an Indian despatch rider section was introduced in divisional signals, followed by a wireless section in 1936.

When World War II commenced in 1939, signal resources were found to be inadequate, as had been the case in World War I. Expansion programmes were put into effect on a war footing, to equip the signal units for campaigns in various theatres. Since British ranks in sufficient numbers could not be made available, some technical trades which had hitherto been their exclusive preserve were opened to Indians. Several new signal units such as army, command, and air formation signals had to be created. These had to be supplied with equipment such as teleprinters, multichannel carrier equipment and long-range wireless sets, about which Indian signallers had virtually no knowledge or experience. To meet the large demand for personnel, recruitment had to be opened to many classes, instead of only four.

An innovation was the raising of the Women's Auxiliary Corps (India) in 1942, consisting of Europeans, Eurasians and Indians. Women cipher operators had been operating in Burma even earlier, and had to be evacuated along with the others after the Japanese invasion. The WAC (I)s were employed throughout the war, as cipher, teleprinter and switchboard operators, and performed magnificently. They were found particularly useful as switchboard operators since most of them were fluent in two languages, including English.

After the end of World War II, the shape of the Corps was very different from what it had been at the beginning. In addition to its normal commitments, the Corps was operating the Defence Telecommunications Network, which had been created during the War and was to be handed over to the Post and Telegraph Department. Due to lack of trained personnel, the P&T Department could not completely take over the network even till mid-1947, and this remained a major commitment for Signals. The Indian Signal Corps now had signal units at General Headquarters, four commands, two districts, four covering forces districts, one armoured, one airborne and three infantry divisions; and also four lines of communication and three air formation signals. In addition there was a large number of training establishments such as the two training centres, at Bangalore and Jubbulpore; the training centre for British ranks and the School of Signals for the Indian Signal Corps at Mhow; and the Army Signal School for regimental signallers at Poona.

Soon after the War ended, it was known that India would soon become independent, and plans were made to 'Indianise' the Army as soon as possible. The initial estimate of the time required for complete Indianisation was nine years, especially for the technical arms, in which certain trades were still manned exclusively by the British. When Lord Mountbatten decided to advance the date of Independence to 15 August 1947, the Army was unprepared, and none so much as the Indian Signal Corps, which had a large number of British officers and other ranks, who could not be replaced at such short notice. Consequently, there was a vacuum when the British left, which could not be filled immediately. As an interim measure British officers were requested to stay on for a few years, and many agreed. One of them was Brigadier C.H.I. Akehurst, the Signal Officer-in-Chief, who continued in this appointment till March 1954. Partition of the country aggravated the problem, since one-third of the manpower, equipment and funds had to be given to the new-born nation of Pakistan. Wherever possible, complete units and establishments were transferred. This included the No. 2 Signal Training Centre at Bangalore.[3]

Signals during Operations
The Indian Signal Corps units took part in every operation undertaken by the Indian Army, before Independence. Barely a year after the first signal companies were raised in 1911, they took part in the Abor Expedition. During World War I, a signal company accompanied each expeditionary force that was sent overseas, and served in every theatre of active operations except Gallipoli and the Balkans. During World War II, Indian signal units served in almost every theatre, except Northern Europe and the Pacific islands.

Between the two Wars, signal units saw active service on numerous operations undertaken by the Indian Army. A summary of active service by the Indian Signal Corps before Independence is given below:[4]

North East Frontier Abor Expedition 1911-12
World War I France 1914-15; Mesopotamia 1914-21; East Africa 1914-17;
Egypt 1914-21; Persia 1915-21; North West Frontier 1914-18

Overseas (1919-39) Kurdistan 1919; Arab Rebellion 1919-22; Aden 1915-27;
Shanghai Defence Force 1927
North East Frontier Kuki Expedition 1918-19

North West Frontier Third Afghan War 1919; Waziristan 1919-20; Mahsud 1919-20
Waziristan 1921-24; Afridi Rebellion 1930-31; Mohmand Bajaur 1933; Loe Agra 1935; Mohmand 1935; Khaisora 1936-36; Waziristan 1937-39.

World War II	Malaya 1939-42; Burma 1939-47; Eritrea 1939-41; North Africa 1942-43; Persia & Iraq 1939-47; Italy 1944-45;
	Greece 1945-46; Malaya 1945-47; Java & Sumatra 1945-46;
	French Indo-China 1945-46; Palestine 1946-47; North West Frontier 1939-47.

Communication Means Used by Signals

Communications involves transportation of information from one point to another. Signals are responsible for military communications, and it is their business to convey information between various echelons and elements of the Army. In a sense, they are like the nervous system in the human body, conveying information between the brain and every limb and organ. Each branch of the Army has its basic weapon or tool of trade, to enable it to perform its task, and so does Signals. The Infantry has its rifles, the Armoured Corps its tanks, and the Artillery its guns. Engineers and Signals differ from others in that they have not one but several tools of trade. However, in many respects, Signals are unique. Signals are ubiquitous and indispensable. There is a saying *"The Government appoints Generals, but Signals make them Commanders."*[5]

Without communications, even the most powerful man is powerless, and his authority extends only to those who can hear his voice. Failure of vital communications can turn victory into defeat, and it is for this reason that Signals are special and treated differently from others. There is a Signals element at every level of command, and even Army and Command Headquarters have their integral signal regiments. Terms such as 'in support', 'in direct support' or 'under command' are never used for Signals—they are always integral, and never diverted, even if not being used in an operation.

Another unique feature of Signals is that it is the only arm that has been authorised reserves, at every level. There are no reserve guns in an artillery battery, reserve tanks in an armoured squadron, or reserve bridges with an engineer regiment. But every signal unit has not only reserve equipment but also reserve detachments, comprising personnel, equipment and vehicles. The reason for this lavish allocation is not difficult to fathom—failure of communications during battle can be catastrophic. No commander likes to take the risk of his communications being disrupted even for a moment, and this is only possible if reserves are close at hand. Another characteristic feature of Signals is the impact of technology. Advances in electronics are more rapid than in any field, and this induces frequent changes in communications media and techniques. Telecommunication equipment becomes obsolescent or obsolete very quickly, and signallers have to constantly update their knowledge and training.

Signallers make use of a wide variety of media, means and systems of communication. From the earliest times till the middle of the nineteenth century, the means were aural, visual or physical. The invention of electric telegraphy, telephony and wireless brought about a revolutionary change in the means of communications. Today, communications are almost entirely based on the transmission of electromagnetic waves. Land-based media can be in the form of open wire lines (permanent line), twisted pair and multicore cables, coaxial cables or optical fibre cable. Radio transmission involving propagation of electromagnetic waves through air, water or space can take the form of radio, radio relay, microwave, troposcatter and satellite communications.

Permanent Line (PL). As the name implies, permanent line (PL) is durable, and lasts for several years. In its simplest form, PL consists of one or more pairs of metal wire strung over poles. O'Shaughnessy constructed the first PL route in India, between 1853 and 1856, for use of the electric telegraph. For the next hundred years, PL was the mainstay of communications, both civil and military. Today, it has been supplanted by microwave, optical fibre and satellite links on major trunk routes, and is used only in rural and isolated areas. The Army continues to use PL in forward areas, especially in the mountains and the eastern sector, where communications are comparatively underdeveloped. In these remote and inhospitable regions, PL has been the backbone of military communications for several decades, though its days are numbered. Old signallers still get a wistful look in their eyes, when they talk about their early days, laying or maintaining PL routes.

Field Cable. Field cable was developed primarily for military use, as the name suggests. It differs from PL in many ways—it is insulated, lighter, and has more than one conductor, making it more flexible. Because of its insulation, field cable can be quickly laid on the ground, while PL has to be strung on poles and takes much longer to construct. It was first used during World War I, to connect various headquarters on telephone. It proved to be a boon by reducing casualties among runners who no longer had to dash about with important messages, even during heavy shelling or machine gun fire. But since the lines were frequently cut, linemen who ventured out to repair them sometimes did not return. In those days, the cable was laid manually, and had to be carried on the back of a man or a mule. Subsequently, horse-drawn cable wagons were designed, which were later replaced by motorised vehicles. A wide variety of reels, drums and cable laying apparatuses were designed, to cater for the different types of field cable. Today there are several types of field cable in use, with better insulation and large number of conductors. One of its greatest assets is versatility—it can be buried, strung on trees or simply left on the ground. Due to its tremendous advantage over radio—security, and immunity to enemy jamming—field cable is the primary means of communication during the defensive phase of battle.

Wireless. The invention of the wireless, now universally called radio, was one of the greatest gifts to mankind. One could literally talk through the air, across continents and oceans. By virtue of the fact that it could be established very quickly, with very little stores and equipment, radio was the ideal means of communication for the military. The earliest sets used spark generators, which were noisy, apart from being large and bulky. The invention of the thermionic valve improved matters, but it was only after the invention of the transistor that radio sets became interference free and small in size. In the initial years, only medium wave signals, in the high frequency (HF) band could be transmitted, using sky wave propagation.

With the growth of technology, the very high frequency (VHF) and ultrahigh frequency (UHF) bands began to be exploited, using line of sight propagation. To increase the range beyond line of sight, signals began to be relayed, giving rise to radio relay transmission. Today, radio and radio relay form important ingredients of communications in the Army.

Though increasing use of radio helped in improving the quality of military communications, it created several concomitant problems. The enemy can monitor radio transmissions and find out the plans of the adversary. To overcome this difficulty, radio telephony procedures were devised, as well as several types of codes and ciphers. Signal intelligence and cryptology are now important aspects of signal communications. Radio signals can also be interfered with or jammed, and if this is done at a crucial juncture, it can create havoc and destruction.[6]

Other means of communication such as Troposcatter, Satellite Communications, Plan AREN and ASCON came into being after the end of World War II and are not discussed here.

The Signal Centre. The signal centre, or signal office as it was known before Independence, is the hub of activity and the nerve centre of a signal unit. Every headquarters, from Army down to brigade, has a signal centre, which functions round the clock, in peace and war. It varies in size, in conformity with the level of the headquarters it supports. The signal centre at Army or Command HQ can occupy a dozen rooms, with scores of people working, while at the brigade it may be housed in a small bunker or tent, with two or three men only. In the field the signal centre is normally in an underground bunker, and during mobile operations, in a vehicle or shelter. It normally works in three shifts, though it is not uncommon to find two shifts in units with additional commitments or shortage of personnel.

The signal centre has several work stations such as Acceptance, Registration, Routing, Circuit, Query and so on, based on the stages through which a message is processed. The crypto centre is also part of the signal centre, though entry to it is restricted to cipher personnel. In large signal centres, each shift has an assistant duty signal officer (ADSO) who is normally an officer, while in smaller ones it may be a JCO. The location of the signal centre is indicated by a 3 feet by 2 feet white and blue flag placed outside on a pole or sticking out of the top of the camouflage net.

The signal centre is a beehive of activity, day or night. There are operators bashing away at keyboards; counter clerks reading messages to confirm that they are legible, signed and bearing the correct precedence and security classification before accepting them for clearance; routing clerks flipping through clearance lists and code sign books; cipher operators coding and decoding messages; mechanics trying to match the speeds of teleprinters at both ends; and the superintendent tongue-lashing a tardy or careless operator. As the number of pending messages pile up, blood pressures and tempers rise, and there is a lot of yelling and shouting, most of it directed at the signal centre staff at the other end. All this time, the ADSO is keeping an eagle eye on the state of circuits to ensure that they are through, and on the state of pending traffic. It is a matter of honour for the shift to hand over with 'no message pending', and defaulters have to face the taunts and jeers of their colleagues in the mess hall and washroom.

The Telephone Exchange. The telephone exchange is normally an adjunct of the signal centre. In peace stations, static exchanges are mostly manned by civilian switchboard operators (CSBOs). These exchanges were earlier hired from the Post and Telegraph Department (P&T) but are now owned by the Army. In the field, ruggedized exchanges of different sizes are used, manned by combatants. In larger exchanges there is a duty exchange officer (DEO) always present, while smaller ones have a supervisor, with the ADSO exercising overall control.

Like the signal centre, the exchange is never silent. More than anywhere else, time is at a premium and the higher the rank of the officer, the shorter the time allowed for his call to be connected. Apart from delayed calls, important subscribers often lose their cool over noisy lines, or for being taken on the line first, if the caller at the other end happens to be junior. Exchange operators are a harassed lot, and many have lost their stripes for being inattentive or discourteous. The exchange has been the Waterloo of many signal officers too, and anecdotes abound about such instances. Not surprisingly, signal officers at all levels always keep the exchange under close watch.[7]

Signal Trades

Being a technical arm, Signals has a large number of trades. The first signal trades were those of lineman and visual signaller which were introduced in 1889 as Sappers and Miners trades. While visual signallers were responsible to man and operate semaphores, the linemen were employed in laying and maintaining light and heavy cable lines. There was no change in the trade structure till 1920 when the trade of lineman was bifurcated into lineman field and lineman permanent line, and the new rank of signalman was introduced. At this time, the composition of signal units was approximately one-third British and two-thirds Indian, the workshop and operator trades being exclusively British. To train Indians in higher technical trades, the Indian Signal Boys' Company was formed in 1933. This was the first such experiment in the Indian Army, and proved highly successful. One of the boys trained under this scheme was Brigadier Mohamed Suleiman, who became Director of Signals of Pakistan.

In 1929 horse-drawn carriages authorised to corps signal units were replaced by motor vehicles, and mechanical transport drivers were transferred to Signals from the Army Service Corps. In 1931 a new trade called signals assistant was introduced. All other ranks were initially trained as signals assistants, and later graded as operator visual or lineman after reporting to units. The birth of yet another trade, the despatch rider, took place during World War I in the British Army. Volunteers came forward to join the new but highly dangerous service, many of them bringing their own machines. They carried messages to the most inaccessible places, at any time of the day or night, during rain or snow. Even enemy shells and machine gun fire did not deter the gallant DRs who soon earned a well-deserved reputation for courage and tenacity in the face of adversity. In 1933 the DR trade was opened to Indians with a good education and equestrian ability. At that time, only Indians from the higher classes could meet both requirements, and there were few takers for the trade. During World War I, executives from business houses of Calcutta and Bombay had volunteered to serve overseas as DRs, using their own motorcycles. When World War II began, Indians formed only forty per cent of the authorised strength of DRs.

Though the proposal to train Indians as operators and instrument mechanics had been considered in 1930, and the boys company formed three years later to achieve this end, it was not until 1938 that Indians were permitted to join the trade of operator telegraphy, electrician (signals) and fitter (signals). During World War II, several other trades were introduced, and a few Indians trained in these. In 1943, two new operator trades were opened to Indians, bifurcating the earlier trade of operator telegraph signals (British). Indians could now become operator telegraph wireless and operator telegraph line. It was only after Independence that Indians were able to join the trades of operator cipher and storeman technical.[8]

Technical trades in Signals are broadly divided into three groups, comprising workshop, operator and lineman categories. The workshop group comprised wireless, line and telegraph mechanics. The operator group had four different combinations of operators who could handle the switchboard and line, wireless and line, keyboard and line, and wireless and keyboard. These were operator wireless and keyboard (OWK), operator wireless and line (OWL), operator switchboard and line (OSL), and operator keyboard and line (OKL). The lineman group has three categories—lineman field, lineman permanent line and lineman test recorder.

In addition to the three basic groups, there are several other technical as well as non-technical trades. The electrician fitter signals (EFS) is primarily responsible for power generators and battery charging; operators cipher man the crypto centre, where messages are coded and decoded; and storekeepers technical looks after all type of technical equipment and stores. The jobs performed by despatch riders has already been described. The draughtsman signals makes the sketches and communication diagrams which are an essential part of every signal instruction. Then there are the clerks who maintain records and documents, and the driver mechanical transport who drives vehicles of various types.

Though most trades in Signals are technical, one must not forget the role of others such as cooks, tailors, washermen, barbers, safaiwalas and equipment repairers. Before Independence, a general class known as camp followers or simply followers performed these jobs. They were not soldiers, and did not take part in actual combat. They provide essential services to personnel in signal units, and are in fact indispensable, because others cannot do their jobs.

A Signaller's Life

The prime responsibility of the Corps of Signals is to provide communications. All activities in signal units and establishments are geared to meet this requirement. As explained earlier, communication involves transmission of information. Signals use a variety of media to transport information between various echelons of the Army. Signallers have to process the information, which is received from users, in the form of messages, to make it suitable for transmission. This may involve encoding, if the information is sensitive. If messages are to be sent over radio, addresses have to be substituted by code signs to maintain secrecy. Incoming messages have to be often retyped, sealed in envelopes, and if the urgency demands, delivered to the addressee by a runner or despatch rider (DR). Signal centres and crypto centres are established by signals at each formation headquarters, to carry out these tasks. They also establish telephone exchanges at every formation headquarters, to facilitate calls between important subscribers. Of course, they lay the lines between the exchanges and the subscribers' premises (a bunker, dugout, shelter or tent) and provide the telephones. During operations, when units and formations move frequently, the lines have to be reeled up, and laid at the next location. The lines are frequently cut due to enemy shelling or by own tanks and vehicles, and have to be repaired, irrespective of the time of the day, weather conditions, and intensity of enemy fire. Signallers never sleep during war, and rarely during peace—the signal centre, crypto centre and telephone exchange function round the clock, in war and peace.

A signaller's life is full of challenge and excitement. Personnel manning the signal centre and exchange are constantly facing unforeseen problems—breakdown in circuits, malfunctions in equipment, delayed message and calls, messages cleared to wrong addresses, traffic pending due to overload, unit moving out and in without informing the signal centre and despatch riders losing their way or meeting with accidents. Line parties have to be frequently sent out to repair lines, in snow and rain. During storms and high winds, antennas can fall or bend, or become misaligned. Lightning often burns up cable and damages exchanges and radio sets. Rain and snow cause 'earths' or short circuits in lines, disrupting communications.

Signallers usually work under pressure because they are always racing against time. Signals have communication yardsticks for almost every type of activity. There are timings laid down for laying a kilometre of cable, erecting an aerial, establishing a signal centre or engineering a radio relay chain. These timings are strictly adhered to, and delays invite immediate reproof from the officer in command. Another case of strain is choleric commanders and sullen staff officers who rarely accept delayed calls and messages even if the reasons are beyond the control of the operators. Often the best method of soothing tempers is to take the concerned officer on a visit to the exchange and signal centre. One look at the bedlam is enough to convince the most irate officer that the operator who did not attend to his call promptly was not sleeping.

Not all signallers work in the signal centre and exchange. There are others who carry out repairs and maintenance of equipment, charge batteries, drive vehicles or perform tasks of an administrative nature. Also, not all signal unit man signal centres and exchanges. There are others which have specified roles or man specialised equipment or systems. There are units which provide communications for air support, air defence and to airfields. There are units which provide troposcatter links and carry out monitoring of radio transmissions not only of the Army but others such as the police and paramilitary forces. There are units especially tasked for carrying out electronic warfare and obtaining signal intelligence. All these units are manned by signallers, who normally serve for three or four years except in high altitude, where the tenure is shorter. Since there is no parent unit system in vogue in the Corps of Signals, personnel are rarely posted to the same unit twice.

Signallers remain busy most of the time, but unit routine is strictly followed. PT and games are held regularly, and so are training activities such as firing on the range, battle physical efficiency tests, route marches by day and night and weekly arms cleaning parades. Technical training is naturally given the highest importance, and regular cadres are held for each trade. Signallers are more fortunate than others in that they are constantly on the job, and this ensures that they are always in a high state of training.

Formation exercises and annual technical training camps provide an opportunity to train under operational conditions, especially to those who don't man static communications in peacetime. Most signallers are educated and highly qualified. They are given opportunities and incentives to obtain higher qualifications, and many acquire graduate and post-graduate degrees that help them in finding a second career after retirement.

How do signallers spend their leisure hours? In the evening, many will be found reading newspapers or books. Study rooms are provided in most units where personnel can study and prepare for examinations even after lights out. Of course, they go to town on 'out pass' on holidays, to see a movie or shop for the family. On religious occasions, everyone attends the celebrations, irrespective of his own beliefs. Signallers participate in social events with gusto and fervour, and the entertainment programmes produced during 'bara khanas' are normally superb.

A signaller must not only be professionally competent, but extremely responsible and trustworthy. In no other arm do other ranks have access to as much information and knowledge as in Signals. Cipher operators handle messages of the highest security, while others in the signal centre deal with signals classified 'Confidential' and below. The Corps of Signals is responsible for crypto systems of all types, including those used by other arms. Exchange and signal centre staff are privy to everything that goes on in the formation, and have to be entirely trustworthy and unimpeachable. Young signalmen with hardly any service have to deal with senior staff officers and formation commanders. They learn to communicate not only with their colleagues at the other end of a line but also with people. The importance of their role inculcates in signallers a sense of pride, confidence and sophistication that is unmatched. All said and done, a signaller's life is worth living, and dying for.⁹

Training

In the Army, there is a popular saying: "Those who sweat in peace don't have to bleed in war." Civilians often wonder what soldiers do in peacetime, and are surprised when told that they train for war. "But surely, you don't need to train each day of the week, all round the year, and for years at a stretch?" they often ask. It may appear incredible, but is the plain truth. One can never train enough for war, and there are many known instances of casualties during battle that can be attributed to deficiencies in training. Sometimes, the result of the engagement itself hinges on the state of training of the adversaries.

Military training can be divided broadly in two parts—unit and institutional. Unit training is the responsibility of the unit commanders, and includes both individual and collective training. Signal units conduct unit training in accordance with annual directives issued by their formation commanders, which are based on policy laid down by Army and Command HQ. Annual training notes are also issued by the Signal Officer-in-Chief, based on which chief signal officers at command and corps HQ issue their own instructions. Adequate resources are provided to unit commanders for carrying out unit training, in the form of funds, equipment, training aids and literature. Military and technical aspects of unit training are supervised through inspections by commanders and chief signal officers. Individual training is normally followed by collective training, in the form of formation exercises, at the level of division, corps or army.

A feature peculiar to Signals is the annual technical training camp, similar to the practice camp of the Artillery. During this camp, the entire unit moves out of its permanent location for about two weeks, and all facets of signalling are practised. An interesting feature of signal training is the 'communication race', in which competing detachments try to pass a message over several types of media, and many stages of processing, in the shortest possible time. Often, the fastest team is not the most accurate, and loses the race due to mistakes committed in coding/decoding or transmission/reception. The communication race brings out very emphatically the importance of teamwork and the need for a balance between speed and accuracy, in accordance with the Corps motto 'Teevra Chaukas' (swift and secure).

Institutional training is carried out at the two signal training centres (STCs) at Jabalpur and Goa, and at the School Of Signals, now known as the Military College of Telecommunication Engineering (MCTE), at Mhow. The STCs are primarily responsible for training recruits, while the MCTE is mainly concerned with officers' training, though it conducts certain specialised courses for others also. The STCs are category 'B' training establishments commanded by brigadiers, and function under the technical control of the Inspectorate of Signals Trade Training (ISTT), which is under the Directorate General of Signals, Army HQ. The MCTE is a category 'A' establishment commanded by a lieutenant general, and functions under the Army Training Command.

Signal Training Centres
The signal training centres of today trace their origin to the Signal Units Depot established at Kirkee in October 1914, for the purpose of holding reinforcements and custody of documents of the signal companies proceeding overseas for active service during World War I. The depot was shifted a few miles to Wanowrie in December 1914, due to shortage of accommodation at Kirkee. It gradually started training visual operators, linemen, and clerks and in 1917 was redesignated as the Signal Service Depot. The depot moved for a few months to Wellington in February 1920, before finally moving to Jabalpur in December 1920. Further redesignations took place in March 1921, when it became the Signal Training Centre and Depot, and in April 1927 when the designation was changed to Signal Training Centre (India).

During World War II, additional training centres came up, and by the end of 1942, there were six centres—two each at Jabalpur and Bangalore, and one each at Rawalpindi and Sialkot. The latter two were disbanded after the war, leaving only the centres Jabalpur and Bangalore. After partition in 1947 the assets of the training centres at Bangalore were transferred to Pakistan. The STCs at Jabalpur and Goa are organised into one military training regiment (MTR) and three technical training regiments (TTR) to impart basic military and technical training to recruits, and to conduct upgradation courses for signal personnel of all trades. Recruits selected for enrolment in the Corps are put through a rigorous regimen of physical training, drill and weapon training at the MTRs for a period of 24 weeks, which transforms the raw and rustic youth into a disciplined, physically fit and mentally alert soldier. After the end of their basic military training the recruits proceed to one of the TTRs for technical training in a specified trade. At the end of the training period the recruits pledge their devotion to duty in the attestation parade and are formally enlisted as trained soldiers. They are then posted to various units in the basic rank of 'Signalman'.[10]

Signals and the Indian National Army
During the Burma campaign in World War II, units of Indian Signals were part of the formations that took part in the operations. This is the time they came to know about the INA that was part of the Japanese forces. Special groups of the INA were being used to carry out espionage and subversion of Indian troops. In the Arakan campaign one of these parties led by Major L.S. Misra managed to subvert an Indian outpost held by a platoon of Gwalior Lancers. The Japanese Air Force was quite active and subjected the forward troops to frequent bombing raids. An interesting system of air raid warning introduced by the Signals unit of 14 Indian Division in March 1943 paid rich dividends. Whenever an enemy plane was spotted over a brigade area, the letters 'A B C' were repeated six times on the fullerphone to the divisional signal office. The signal master immediately informed the 'G Ops' branch who ordered own aircraft to take off. Three enemy planes were shot down by this method. Sometimes, the Japanese planes dropped pamphlets that were addressed to Indian soldiers, exhorting them to join the Indian National Army. These were written in Roman Hindustani,

which could be understood by Indian soldiers. These pamphlets disparaged Anglo-American aspirations and the efforts of Mahatma Gandhi to achieve independence by non-violent means. A typical pamphlet along with the English translation is reproduced below:[11]

> **"HINDOSTANI SIPAHION KE LIE."**
>
> Tum kion larne ke lie ae ho? Kya tum apna khoon Anglo-Americano ke gulamon ke haisiat se bahana chahte ho? Jaise kih ret ke thaile Anglo-Americano ka bachao karte hain. Nahin, Nahin! abhi waqt nahin guzra. Anglo-Americano ke paharedaron ki haisiat se apni qurbani mat karo. Tumhare bhaion ne Hindostan men Anglo-Americano khilaf shaqt bagawat shuru kar di hai. East men bhi Hindustani sipahion ne jin ki bhi tumhari hi jaisi halat thi sachche desh bhakton ka farz ada karne ke lie aur Hindostan ki azadi ke lie Indian National Army qaem karli hai. Unhon ne Hindustan ki taraf barhna shuru kar dia hai.
>
> **HINDUSTANI SIPAHIO AO, AUR HAMARE SATH MIL JAO!**
> **INDIAN NATIONAL ARMY MEN SHAMIL HO JAO!**

"FOR INDIAN SOLDIERS"

"Why have you come to fight? Do you want to spill your blood like slaves of the Anglo-Americans? Like the sandbags that protect the Anglo-Americans. No, No! There is still time. Do not sacrifice your lives like the sentries of the Anglo-Americans. Your brothers have begun the revolt against the Anglo-Americans in India. In the East too Indian soldiers who were in a situation similar to yours have acted like true patriots and established the Indian National Army in order to gain freedom for India. They have started advancing towards India.

INDIAN SOLDIERS, COME AND JOIN US!
JOIN THE INDIAN NATIONAL ARMY!"

Another pamphlet gave directions to Indian soldiers who wanted to cross over to the INA. It was written in Roman Hindustani as well as Japanese. It carried the signature of the Commander-in-Chief Nippon Army (Japanese Army) as well as the Commander-in-Chief Indian National Army. It advised those who had this leaflet to come towards the

Japanese or INA forces, with a white flag or with raised hands, with the muzzles of their weapons pointing downwards. They were assured that they will be welcomed properly and given respect.

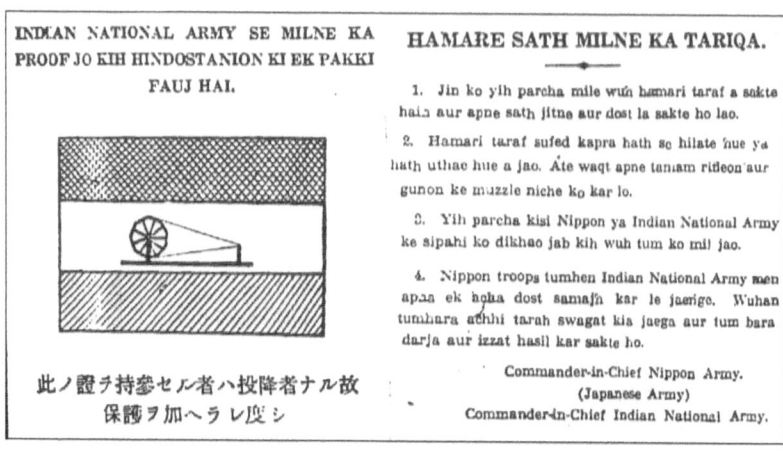

Along with other Indian soldiers who joined the INA after being captured by the Japanese, several men from Signals also did so. According to available records, 110 personnel of the Indian Signal Corps had joined the INA. Of these, 56 were in India and 54 in Pakistan after Partition. Twelve of the INA personnel in India were re-enrolled in the Army. However, only five joined Signals, the rest going to other regiments. Two were re-enrolled in ASC, three in Border Scouts, one in the Artillery and one in the EME. Some of them had joined the INA against their will, or as a means to improve their chances of escape. Their stories make interesting reading. One such individual was Havildar E.D. Thomas, who was part of 12 Indian Infantry Brigade Signal Company, which was captured by the Japanese in Malaya in January 1942. The two officers in the signal section, Major T.A.K. Howe and Captain A.C. Iyappa were also captured at the same time.

According to Thomas, he was captured at Kalap Bali Estate on 8 January 1942. He crossed the Slim River and escaped in the thick jungle, only to be caught by the Japanese after five days. He was sent to the POW Camp at Anderson School, Ipoh, where he remained for six months. He was then sent to the Seletav Camp in Malaya, where he spent another two months. Apparently, he joined the INA because of the bad food and in order to improve his chances of escape. He claims to have obtained the permission of Captain Iyappa, which appears doubtful. He was sent to the Akyab Front, and was captured by an American unit (686 AAA) when the Japanese retreated from Akyab to Meiktila. Because of his education and experience, he was employed by the Americans as a storekeeper and clerk, staying with the unit for several months in Magwe. He fell sick with malaria and dysentery, and stayed with a Hindu family in the village when the Americans left, giving him some money. When he recovered, he travelled to Rangoon and reported to an Indian unit (226 BOD) where he worked for a few months. After he had saved enough money to pay for a voyage home, he returned to his home in Mysore in January 1947.

Thomas was captured in Malaya in January 1942 and returned to India after five years, in January 1947. Except for about eight months in the Japanese POW camp and a few months with the American unit in Magwe, in the middle of 1945 (he has two testimonials, dated 8 and 16 May 1945, given to him by Captain Michal Filipith and Robert C. Morthey of 686 AAA of the US Army), it is not clear where he spent the rest of his epic journey. After reaching home, he applied to the OC, Signal Training Battalion, STC Jubbulpore, expressing his desire to join the Army again, or at least for a discharge certificate so that he could find alternate employment. In view of his long absence from duty, it is doubtful if his request was granted.[12]

Notes
1. Brig T. Barreto, *History of the Corps of Signals*, vol. I, (revised edition) (New Delhi: The Corps of Signals Association, 2006), p. 33.
2. Brig T. Barreto, *History of the Corps of Signals*, vol. I (revised edition) (New Delhi: The Corps of Signals Association, 2006), p. 63.
3. *Through – Saga of the Corps of Signals* (New Delhi: The Corps of Signals Association, Brijbasi Art Press, 2001), p. 26.
4. *Through – Saga of the Corps of Signals* (New Delhi: The Corps of Signals Association, Brijbasi Art Press, 2001), pp. 28-30.
5. *Through – Saga of the Corps of Signals* (New Delhi: The Corps of Signals Association, Brijbasi Art Press, 2001), p. 42.

6. *Through – Saga of the Corps of Signals* (New Delhi: The Corps of Signals Association, Brijbasi Art Press, 2001), p. 48.
7. *Through – Saga of the Corps of Signals* (New Delhi: The Corps of Signals Association, Brijbasi Art Press, 2001), p. 56.
8. *Through – Saga of the Corps of Signals* (New Delhi: The Corps of Signals Association, Brijbasi Art Press, 2001), p. 60.
9. *Through – Saga of the Corps of Signals* (New Delhi: The Corps of Signals Association, Brijbasi Art Press, 2001), p. 68.
10. *Through – Saga of the Corps of Signals* (New Delhi: The Corps of Signals Association, Brijbasi Art Press, 2001), p. 74.
11. *War Diary*, 14 Indian Divisional Signals.
12. Brig T. Barreto, *History of the Corps of Signals*, vol. I (revised edition) (New Delhi: The Corps of Signals Association, 2006), pp. 312-14.

5
The Army (Signals) Mutiny at Jubbulpore—1946

In February 1946, there was a mutiny at the Signal Training Centre of the Indian Army at Jubbulpore (now called Jabalpur). It was by no means the first such incident in the Indian Army. Some of the prominent mutinies in the Indian Army during British rule were the Vellore Mutiny (1806); the Barrackpore Mutiny (1824); the Great Indian Mutiny (1857); the Singapore Mutiny (1915); the Peshawar Mutiny (1930); the Suez Canal Army Revolt (1943); the Ambala Cantt. Army Revolt (1943); and the Jhansi Regiment Case (1940).

The mutiny at Jubbulpore took place between 27 February and 3 March 1946, about two weeks after the Naval mutiny at Bombay. The men who participated in the mutiny were all Indian Signal Corps personnel posted at the Signal Training Centre. According to official sources, 1,716 men were involved in the mutiny. The immediate provocation for the revolt was the firing on the naval ratings at Bombay and the harsh punishments awarded to the INA prisoners after the trials at the Red Fort. The men also had certain grievances concerning pay, food and accommodation that they placed before their superior officers and were agitated when these were not heard. The uprising was peaceful and the participants did not resort to violence of any kind. Like the naval mutiny at Bombay and Karachi, the Jubbulpore revolt was put down with an iron hand, by using British troops. There was no firing, but a bayonet charge that left about 70 men injured, and three dead.

Though the mutiny at Jubbulpore was at that time not considered as 'serious' as the Naval mutiny, its repercussions were immense. The earlier revolts in the RIAF and RIN, though more widespread and larger in scale, did not really worry the British authorities, because the Indian Army, on which they depended for meeting external and internal threats, was still considered reliable, having proved its fidelity during World War II. The mutiny at Jubbulpore was the first major uprising in the Indian Army during or after the war. This set alarm bells ringing from Delhi to London, and doubts began to be expressed on the steadfastness of the Indian Army. Ultimately, it forced Britain to reach a settlement with the political parties and quit India.

After the end of World War II there was a feeling of uncertainty among soldiers, with the threat of demobilisation and loss of livelihood being matters of serious concern. The return of a large number of troops from British colonies in South-East Asia aggravated the situation, with military stations in India overwhelmed with troops for whom there was little work and no accommodation. This led to severe overcrowding and a fall in standards of hygiene, food and discipline, the latter due to lack of employment. During the war, most of the men had been serving in operational areas, remaining ignorant or unaware of the political situation in the country. The demands for independence from British rule escalated after the 1942 Quit India agitation, and the end of the war raised expectations in the minds of the public that freedom was imminent. Most of the men went home on leave for the first time after the war, and learned of the momentous political events that had taken place during the last three or four years. The INA trials also played a part in kindling among soldiers 'political consciousness', of which they had no earlier experience.

In February 1946, there were two major establishments of the Indian Signal Corps at Jubbulpore. The first was the Signal Training Centre (STC) comprising No. 1 Signal Training Battalion (Military) and 2 & 3 Signal Training Battalions (Technical). The second was the Indian Signal Depot & Records, which comprised the Indian Signals Depot, the Indian Signals Demobilisation Centre and the Indian Signals Records. The Commandant of the STC was Colonel L.C. Boyd, while Colonel R.T.H. Gelston commanded the Depot & Records. Both these establishments came under the Jubbulpore Area, commanded by Brigadier H.U. Richards, who also commanded 17 Indian Infantry Brigade. The Area came under the General Officer Commanding Nagpur District, Major General F.H. Skinner, with his headquarters at Nagpur. Headquarters Central Command was then located at Agra.

Conditions at Jubbulpore were no different from those at other military stations, except that the men, being mostly from technical trades, were more educated. Many of the men undergoing long training courses were not sure whether they would be retained or sent home in the next few months. The delay in announcement of a clear policy on demobilisation had created an air of uncertainty and restlessness, which could not remain unnoticed. On 27 November 1945, Colonel Boyd had written to the Organisation Directorate in General Headquarters (India), bringing this to their notice. He wrote:[1]

> It is for consideration whether the present policy of continuing to put men under lengthy courses of training, irrespective of the time they are likely to remain in the Army, is not extremely wasteful both of instructors' time and Government.... Among these men unsettlement and lack of interest in their work are already noticeable, since they think they will be released from the Army before their course finishes. It should also be noted that it is the highly educated men such as are enrolled for Group 'A' trades that are keenest to leave the Army at the earliest possible moment in order to obtain highly remunerative employment.... To carry on with Workshops and Operator training in these circumstances seems to be a waste of time. The unsettlement in squads already referred to is having an adverse effect on training ...

It was almost three months before General Headquarters (India), replied to Colonel Boyd's letter, ordering the immediate release of one thousand recruits then under training at the Indian Signal Training Centre at Jubbulpore and Bangalore.[2]

By the time the orders reached the STC the mutiny had broken out. Referring to the letter in his report to the Area Headquarters after the mutiny, Colonel Boyd lamented: *'It is unfortunate that the decision contained therein could not have been come to earlier'.*³

Even if the decision to release the thousand men had been taken earlier, it would have been difficult for the Signal Training Centres to cope with such large numbers. The Signals Depot was then not authorised a demob centre; it was making do with an ad hoc demob centre that had a capacity to release only 70 persons in a day. The staff of the depot was already overworked and the additional load would have stretched them to the limit. The severe overcrowding and unsatisfactory living conditions only added to the unrest. The shortage of staff affected management of security in the area, and the men had free access to civilian areas. The Signal Training Centre, Depot and Records employed large numbers of civilians, through whom political developments found their way into the military camp and the idle minds of the men, easily converting them into 'devil's workshops'.

At that time, units were given cash to purchase condiments, which were not being supplied with rations. There had been a delay in purchase of condiments with the resultant deterioration in the quality of food being prepared in the *langars* (Other Ranks messes in the Indian Army are generally called thus. The term is taken from the free kitchen in a *gurudwara*, the place of worship for Sikhs). The personnel responsible for purchasing condiments were often corrupt, and the quantity and quality of condiments was much below the prescribed standards. This applied also to the rations supplied to the men through the supply depot manned by the Royal Indian Army Service Corps. Other than rations, even other stores and amenities authorised to the men were frequently pilfered. The general standard of the men's cookhouses, living quarters, bathrooms and urinals was poor. Unlike in operational units, there was very little contact between the officers and the men, whose grievances often went unnoticed or were ignored. The quality of Viceroy's Commissioned Officers (VCOs) and Non-Commissioned Officers (NCOs) posted in instructional appointments in the STC was usually good, but the same could not be said of the supervisory staff responsible for administration, some of whom had been in Jubbulpore for several years, developing a callous attitude towards the men and their problems.

A feature unique to technical arms such as the Indian Signal Corps was the presence of a large number of British soldiers in every unit and establishment. Before the war, most of the technical trades in the Indian Signal Corps were open only to British Other Ranks (BOR), with Indian Other Ranks being eligible for the 'lower' trades such as operator visual, despatch rider, lineman, MT driver, etc. Before the war, the Indian Signal Corps comprised about two thousand BOR, with the number of IOR being almost twice that number. When the war ended, the number of BOR had gone up ten times to almost twenty thousand, while the number of IOR had grown thirty times to sixty thousand. The rapid expansion of the Corps necessitated several new trades being opened to Indians, who began to be recruited as mechanics, operators and electricians. By the end of the war Indians were employed in all jobs that were being done earlier by Europeans, the exception being ciphers, which was not opened to Indians until Independence. Though IOR were now doing the same job as BOR, there was considerable disparity in their status—BOR did not salute Viceroy's Commissioned Officers (VCOs)—salaries, rations and living conditions. This naturally irked the Indians, who saw no reason for this discrimination.

A seemingly inconsequential cause for discontent was the bad quality of *gur* (jaggery) being supplied to the troops by resorting to local purchase. This had been officially reported to the Centre Headquarters on 25 February 1946. However, the decision on the complaint or the progress was not communicated to the men. On 26 February a number of notices were seen pasted on the company notice boards in the lines of the Demob Centre and No. 4 Depot Company. Some notices had 'Jai Hind' written on them, while others called upon all Indian Other Ranks to cease work and, if necessary, shed blood. The notices were seen in the morning by Lieutenant Colonel E.W. Anderson, Officer Commanding Indian Signals Depot, who reported this to the Commandant, Colonel R.T.H. Geltson. Viewing the situation as serious, Colonel Gelston immediately sought an interview with the Area Commander, to report on an 'Intelligence' matter. At 3 p.m., Colonel Gelston and Lieutenant Colonel Anderson met the Area Commander and apprised him of the notices. In the evening, all officers were called for a conference and explained the developments. At about 6 p.m. all IOR of Records were paraded and the Company Commander, Captain D.S. Garewal, addressed them, in the presence of Lieutenant Colonel Anderson and the Officer in Charge Records, Lieutenant Colonel C.M. Macdonald. The men were calm during the address, and there was no untoward incident.

The mutiny started at about 9.20 a.m. on 27 February 1946 in 'G' Company of No. 2 Signal Training Battalion. The first works parade was held at 7 a.m. as usual, and the men were drilled. All officers attended the parade which ended at about 8.30 a.m., when everyone broke off for breakfast. Soon after breakfast, about 200 men, mainly workshop trainees, formed up in the lines of the unit, just before the second works parade was due to fall in. Most of them were in uniform, carrying flags of the Congress and Muslim League. They formed a procession and marched out of the unit, shouting slogans of 'Jai Hind' and 'Inquilab Zindabad'. The Senior Viceroy Commissioned Officer of the unit, Subedar Major and Honorary Captain Ahmed Khan, asked them to halt, but they did not listen to him. Khan immediately telephoned the Adjutant, who was having breakfast in the Officers Mess. The Adjutant told the Subedar Major that Major C.C. Tucker, the officiating Commanding Officer, had left the mess about five minutes earlier and he should await his arrival in the office. He also informed Major D.C. Dashfield and Captain J. Knowles, Company Commander and Training Officer respectively of 'G' Company, who were in the mess with him. Collecting another officer, Captain M.B. Myers, they left for the unit area on bicycles.

Information about the crowd collecting and shouting slogans in front of the guard room of No. 2 Signal Training Battalion had also reached Colonel Gelston, whose office was located just a hundred yards away. Gelston saw the crowd leave the unit area and move along Peter's Path, which led towards No. 3 Signal Training Battalion and the Signals Depot. He telephoned the Area Headquarters and also the Depot, warning them that that the crowd might come that way. The Depot Commander, Lieutenant Colonel Anderson, was then in his bungalow. When Gelston rang him up, he told him that he had called for a 15-cwt. vehicle and was planning to come to his office, to report that notices had again been seen during the morning parade. Gelston informed Anderson of the developments, and asked him to pick him up from his office, so that they could both go and see what was happening.

Meanwhile, the procession was proceeding on Peter's Path, along Napier Road to the lines of No. 3 Signal Training Battalion. Major Tucker was cycling to his office when he met the crowd. Having failed in his attempt to stop them, he cycled ahead and warned No. 3 Signal Training Battalion of their approach. The four officers of No. 2 Signal Training Battalion had also reached the unit, and the Adjutant telephoned No. 3 Signal Training Battalion. Major Dashfield and Captain Knowles got into a 3-ton lorry and drove towards the crowd at full speed. Having been warned of the approach of the procession, No. 3 Signal Training Battalion had turned out its guard. But the crowd brushed it aside, and entered the unit area, sweeping Major Tucker off his bicycle. When Major Dashfield and Captain Knowles caught up with him, he ordered them to go after the crowd and halt them. Noticing that the crowd was about to leave 3 Signal Training Battalion near the Boys' Company, they halted the truck and went towards the mob. When Major Dashfield asked them to stop, one of them said, 'we have demands'. Captain Knowles, who had his back towards the crowd, was hit three times by stones. Enveloping the officers, the crowd continued on its way.

Colonel Gelston and Lieutenant Colonel Anderson reached the crowd as they were coming out of No. 3 Signal Training Battalion. They were soon joined by Major Dashfield and Captain Knowles. The four officers got out of their vehicles and tried to stop the men, who just rushed past them and marched through the Depot. They were very excited and seemed completely out of hand, shouting slogans and waving party flags. Lieutenant Colonel Anderson kept moving with the head of the column while Colonel

Gelston got in the truck and asked the driver to start. The truck was soon surrounded by the mutineers and some even tried to get in. Gelston ordered the driver to keep moving forward slowly. At one stage the driver's foot slipped off the pedal and the truck bounded forward, knocking over two men. Due to the heavy rush, even Anderson was almost run over. After this, the truck was stopped and Anderson got in. Both officers then made their way to the Depot.

Realising that they would not be able to stop the procession on their own, Lieutenant Colonel Anderson collected about 15 men and issued them with rifles. He also armed Dashfield and Knowles with pistols and the party moved in a lorry towards the procession, which had already passed through the Depot. Overtaking the crowd on the Outram Road about 200 yards from the Nerbudda Junction, they halted the lorry with the men keeping their rifles at the aim. The officers dismounted and Anderson threatened to shoot if the men did not stop. Hearing this, the men in the crowd bared their chests and dared him to open fire. The three officers were literally thrust out of the way and the crowd turned off the Nerbudda Road towards Gorakhpur and headed for the city.

Two Viceroy's Commissioned Officers of 'G' Company followed the crowd and attempted to find out their complaints. The main grievances of the men were:[4]

- Differences in pay between IORs & BORS.
- Poor quality of rations.
- Why was fire opened on RIN ratings?
- Why were two INA officers sentenced to seven years RI when others were merely cashiered?

Undeterred by the attempts to stop them the crowd proceeded towards the city. Having reached Tilak Bhumi, Tillaya, they stopped and held a meeting, where speeches were made by some of the men highlighting their grievances. There was a lot of slogan shouting and waving of flags of Congress and Muslim League. Some of them went to the local office of the Congress Party and sought the help of the local political leaders.

An officer from the Intelligence Branch of Area Headquarters and some officers from the Signal Training Centre also went to the venue in civil dress and noted down the names of the prominent persons taking an active part in the meeting and discussions.

The news of the incident spread quickly. There was considerable tension in the city and shopkeepers closed their shops. However, the meeting was peaceful and there was no violence or unruly behaviour by the men. At about 4.15 p.m. they started back for the unit. By this time the military authorities had mobilised two companies of 27th (Garrison) battalion of the 9th Jat Regt and two ID (Internal Disturbance) companies of the Signal Training Centre in case force was required to carry out arrests. But the crowd entered the lines peacefully and sat down in the battalion area. The troops earmarked for effecting arrests were therefore asked to stand down. The ID companies, which had taken over the main guard, *kot* (armoury) and magazine guard were later relieved by the Jat troops. The 'ring-leaders', whose names had been noted down by the Area Intelligence Officer and by other officers from Signal Training Centre, were asked to fall out when their names were called, which they did without any protest. Major C.C. Tucker, the officiating Commanding Officer of No. 2 Signal Training Battalion, ordered a Viceroy's Commissioned Officer to march the ringleaders to the main quarter guard. Sensing what was going to happen next, the others pulled them back into the crowd.

Soon afterwards, the Commandant, Colonel L.C. Boyd arrived, followed by the Area Commander, who addressed the men. He told them that they were all under arrest, but assured them that he would forward their grievances to higher authorities. They fell in and were marched to the Signal Training Centre Cage where the Commandant noted down their demands, which were as under:[5]

- Increase of basic pay.
- Increase of rations.
- Better accommodation.
- Equal treatment with British Other Ranks.
- Speedier demobilisation.

- Protest against speeches of the Commander-in-Chief and Admiral Godfrey—the passage that if Indian Army soldiers are indisciplined every force would be used against them.
- Release of all INA prisoners including Captain Rashid and Burhanuddin.
- Unnecessary to spend one crore on Victory celebrations when there is food crisis in India.
- Ready to work if the demands are put forward. We did no indiscipline while out. Pray no action against us.

After taking down their grievances the Commandant spoke to the men and left. When the afternoon parade was dismissed a number of men of No. 2 Signal Training Battalion approached the Cage and started milling around shouting words of encouragement. Those who wished to join their friends inside the Cage were allowed to do so and the rest were ordered to return, which they did. After dark the same thing occurred. The men inside the Cage refused food and bedding. When the Commandant came to know of this he entered the Cage and spoke to the men, after which they agreed to eat food and accepted bedding. Apart from sporadic slogans, the night passed without incident.

By early next morning, a British battalion, the Somerset Light Infantry had arrived in Jubbulpore. A party of about 80 men from No. 2 Signal Training Battalion assembled in the unit at 7 a.m. and began moving along the same route that had been taken by their colleagues on the previous day, but before they could cover any substantial distance, they were intercepted by a platoon of the British battalion. When addressed by various officers, a few of them agreed to return to work but the remainder were left on the roadside under the guard of British troops.

At 9 a.m. No. 2 Signal Training Battalion was paraded. Major Tucker and Colonel Boyd addressed the men and asked them to return to work. Though the men remained orderly they refused, saying that they could not do so because their comrades were in custody. If they were let out, they would all go back to work. They were asked to return to their lines and remain quiet, which they readily agreed to do. At about 10 a.m. personnel of No. 3 Signal Training Battalion became restive, and about 100 men joined the clerks of the Records and sat down with them, demanding the release of the men inside the Cage. Some officers and Viceroy's Commissioned Officers tried to talk them out of this demand, but very few responded. A few men from the ID companies who had been asked to stand down took off their equipment and joined the crowd.

The District Commander, Major General Skinner arrived to get a first-hand account of the events. In consultation with the Area Commander and the Commandant Signal Training Centre, a plan was made to arrest the ringleaders. The officiating Commanding Officer and the Subedar Major would enter the cage to reason with the men and try to effect the arrests placidly. If this were to fail, then the ringleaders would be pointed out to the Company Commander of the Somerset Light Infantry, who would make the arrests forcibly. Major Tucker, Lieutenant Waugh and Subedar Major Khan entered the Cage and reasoned with the men for over an hour without success. The Second-in-Command of 27 Jat and Lieutenant Colonel Poonoose, an Indian officer who had been called from Katni, then entered the Cage and spent another hour, but failed to induce the ringleaders to give themselves up. There was no recourse left except the use of force.

About 80 soldiers of the Somerset Light Infantry entered the Cage, with bayonets fixed on their rifles. A few of the men were physically removed, amidst a lot of shouting. Faced with the bayonets of the British troops, the crowd retreated to one corner of the cage, which gave way under the weight of sheer numbers. A large number managed to escape through the gap, while the remainder were involved in a scuffle with the British troops. Many sustained injuries from bayonets and some were trampled in the stampede. The injured were immediately removed to the hospital. Some of the men who escaped rushed towards the city but others who were very frightened hid in huts in the lines or in the local countryside. Information about the escapees was conveyed to the police and the civil authorities, with a request to arrest them and bring them back at the earliest.

The news of the bayonet charge spread like wildfire in the Signal Training Centre and at many places the men came out and demonstrated against this, resulting in some more arrests. At 6 p.m. 14 men returned voluntarily, followed by some more in smaller groups of two or three. They were all placed under arrest and put in the guardroom. At about 7.30 p.m. information was received from the local police that about 200 men who had been rounded up by them were being returned in police lorries. The District Commander and Commandant Signal Training Centre met these men when they arrived. The injured were sent to the hospital while the rest were sent to the Jat lines. Meanwhile, about 100 men of No. 3 Signal Training Battalion continued to sit in the Records lines.

While events had taken a serious turn in the Signal Training Centre on 28 February 1946, things were far from normal in the Depot and Records. In the morning about 200 clerks of the Records collected near 4 Company lines and marched towards the Depot Battalion. The Commanding Officer, Lieutenant Colonel Anderson, turned out his Internal Defence Company and followed them, accompanied by his Second-in-Command and Captain D.S. Garewal of Signals Records. They met the crowd of mutineers on the bridge near the Indian Military Hospital. A column of the Somerset Light Infantry had also arrived and was lined up on the Outram Road opposite the hospital. Lieutenant Colonel Anderson spoke to the men and asked them what they wanted. On being told that they had several grievances he asked them to return to their lines and hand over their grievances, which he promised to take up with the authorities. After some hesitation they agreed and followed him to the lines, where they sat down and narrated their grievances, which were noted down and handed over to the Area Commander when he arrived soon afterwards to address the men. Lieutenant Colonel Anderson again spoke to the men and asked them to return to work but they refused.

A company of the Somerset Light Infantry had been placed around the lines of No. 4 Company. With the help of some British soldiers, the Brigade Major of 17 Indian Infantry Brigade, Major K.B. Langdon, arrested four Indian Other Ranks who were then marched away. After these arrests and the departure of the Area Commander, about 100 men of No. 3 Signal Training Battalion rushed into the 4 Company lines and joined the mutineers, accompanied by a lot of shouting. Lieutenant Colonel C. M. Macdonald, the Officer-in-Charge Records and Captain Macfarlane, Adjutant No. 3 Signal Training Battalion tried to quieten the men. After about ten minutes the newly arrived recruits sat down behind the mutineers already seated there. Some more officers from No. 3 Signal Training Battalion arrived and tried to persuade their men to return to their lines but failed. The total number of mutineers present in No. 4 Company had now swelled to almost 350. The Commandant Indian Signals Depot and Records, Colonel Gelston spoke to them about their grievances and promised to do all that could be done to remove them. The men also demanded the release of the four men arrested earlier and the removal of British troops. At 4 p.m. the British troops were withdrawn without any visible reaction from the mutineers. The night of 28 February passed off without any further incident.

In the early hours of 1 March 1946, about 150 Other Ranks from 3 Signal Training Battalion left their lines and marched in a procession towards Sadar Bazar, shouting slogans and waving flags. This information was conveyed to Area Headquarters, which ordered a company from Somerset Light Infantry to proceed to the garrison ground, where the crowd was reported to have headed for. At 7.30 a.m. the Commanding Officer, Lieutenant Colonel R.B.S. Eraut, the Adjutant, Captain Facfarlane and Jemadar Natesan, a Madrassi Mussalman interpreter, proceeded to the Garrison Ground but found no trace of the procession. Colonel Eraut went to the Area Headquarters, while Captain Facfarlane and Jemadar Natesan searched for the crowd in the city and the cantonment, without success. On their return to the unit they discovered that 24 men from the Internal Disturbance Company had joined the procession. The Commanding Officer ordered the Internal Disturbance Company to stand down, and the British guard to take over.

At about 9 a.m. information was received that the procession was coming back in an endeavour to mobilise the remainder of the unit. The Commanding Officer positioned a few officers and Viceroy's Commissioned

Officers to meet the procession when it reached the lines and divert them to the football ground. The Commandant reached the unit shortly before the arrival of the procession at 9.45 a.m. Efforts to guide them to the football ground failed and they moved towards the staging camp. They were stopped en route and the Commanding Officer began to address them. At first he was shouted down but eventually succeeded in making them sit down and listen. The Commandant then addressed the men and listened to their points. Since it was the morning break, the rest of No. 3 Signal Training Battalion also gathered round to listen. After the Commandant left for the Area Headquarters, the Commanding Officer ordered the unit to parade for normal work. This order was not immediately obeyed but after about twenty minutes all the men less the demonstrators returned to work. At about 11.30 a.m. Lieutenant Colonel Poonoose arrived and addressed the men for over an hour, after which a few of them returned to work. It appeared that many more were willing but were being prevented by the leaders.

At about 13.15 p.m. the Subedar Major reported to the Commanding Officer that the demonstrators were requesting permission to go to the cook house and have their food, and promised to return to normal duties after that. The Commanding Officer agreed making it clear that the normal course of military law would be followed. Shortly after this the Subedar Major accompanied by 11 men left for the Records lines in order to persuade the party of mutineers from No. 3 Signal Training Battalion who were sitting there to return. He came back after 30 minutes and reported that he had not only failed in convincing the mutineers but had lost two men of his party, who had been persuaded to join them. After lunch, all the men except for those still in Records attended the afternoon works parade.

The situation in No. 4 Company of Records on 1 March continued to be tense. Captain Garewal, the Company Commander attended the first works parade at 8 a.m. and found only two men present. The mutineers were still sitting between the first and second barracks, where they had been the previous day. Most of them were seated in orderly ranks, with a few standing around and talking. At about 10.30 a.m. they became noisy and began to form a procession, taking down several Congress and Muslim League flags from the open ground between the barracks and the road where they had been erected the previous day. However, there were many among them who shouted to the men to stay in the lines, and the procession broke up into small groups. At about midday the flags were re-erected. Shortly afterwards a deputation led by the Subedar Major of No. 3 Signal Training Battalion arrived to persuade their men to return. There was a heated discussion followed by a lot of pulling and pushing, and some men were physically prevented from going back.

At the second works parade, not a single man fell in on the parade ground. The Officer-in-Charge Records was informed that some men would go to work individually but were afraid to come to the parade ground. At about 4.15 p.m., Colonel Gelston and Lieutenant Colonel Poonoose arrived and met the men. Poonoose spoke to the men with all officers present, and later alone. At 5.45 p.m., Colonel Gelston and Lieutenant Colonel Poonoose left to meet the Area Commander. At the Roll Call parade at 6 p.m., 41 men were present. The rest of the men were still sitting between the two barracks, but were quiet.

The previous day's incidents had been reported in several newspapers and there was considerable resentment at the bayonet charge on the Indian soldiers. According to the newspapers, three men had been killed, while 70 were injured in the bayonet charge. The District Magistrate, Mr. E.S. Hyde declared Jubbulpore Cantonment a restricted area, and the entry of civilians was banned. Notices to this effect were pasted at prominent places and also announced by the beat of drum. Headquarters Jubbulpore Area had also issued instructions confining all troops to lines. Another infantry battalion, the First Royal Gurkha Rifles (1 RGR) had also arrived.

On 2 March 1946, Lieutenant Colonel Poonoose again spoke to the mutineers in Records and No. 3 Signal Training Battalion. He reported that he had failed to make any headway and found that some men who had appeared to be amenable the previous day were now obdurate. During the day, a message from Major General F.H. Skinner, General Officer Commanding Nagpur District was read out to all ranks, in English and

Urdu. Making it clear that the action of the men who had collectively absented themselves from their lines without permission amounted to mutiny, it went on to assure that there would be no mass punishment and *"justice would be tempered with mercy"*. The message also appreciated the conduct of those who had remained staunch to their duty in the *"face of provocation and bad example"*.[6]

During the day, conditions improved. In No. 2 Signal Training Battalion, all men reported for the first works parade except for nine, who also reported after half an hour. In No. 3 Signal Training Battalion all men resumed duties except for the 100 men in Records and those detained in the Jat lines. Major Dashfield visited the Jat lines with some Viceroy's Commissioned Officers and tried to bring back some of the men, but they refused to come unless the ringleaders were released as well.

At 12.30 p.m., Captain Garewal read out the District Commander's message, twice in Urdu and once in English, using a public address system. Everyone heard this in silence. During the afternoon, all was quiet and there was no shouting of slogans. At the evening roll call, 268 men were present. At 9 p.m., the mutineers announced that they were willing to end the mutiny. They burned their flags and started reporting at the office, where their names were noted down. The 100 men of No. 3 Signal Training battalion returned to their lines. By 11 p.m., it appeared that all mutineers had surrendered, except the ones in the Jat lines.

On 3 March 1946 a roll call parade was held in all units at 9 a.m. Immediately afterwards some ringleaders were arrested and sent to the Jat lines. Troops of 17 Indian Infantry Brigade had placed a cordon around the lines. The Area Commander and Commandant Signal Training Centre visited the mutineers in the Jat lines. They said that they were willing to come back if all of them were released. The ringleaders among them had been segregated and without them the others refused to return to their units.

During the next two days, the situation improved, but was still far from normal. The men in the Jat lines refused to come out until their leaders were released. There were no incidents on 4 and 5 March and normal parades were held in the units. On 7 March all the men in the Jat lines returned. On reaching their units they staged a protest for the release of the ringleaders, threatening to go on strike again if this was not done. However, the threat did not materialise and there were no untoward incidents after 7 March 1946. The mutiny was over.

The mutiny had shocked the military establishment, especially the British officers who had always believed that the Indian soldier would never rebel. The reasons for the disaffection were quickly analysed and remedial measures taken. The District Commander issued instructions to all concerned to improve the standard of food and accommodation. Lieutenant Colonel Cassani from the Welfare General's Branch visited the lines of the Indian Signals Depot on 6 March 1946 and submitted a detailed report at General Headquarters (India). The report brought to light the pathetic conditions under which the Indian troops lived. After it was found that some officers, Viceroy's commissioned officers and non-commissioned officers had spent almost eight to ten years at Jubbulpore, those who had been there for over two years were immediately posted out. The number of Indian officers was increased, so that they could understand the problems of Indian troops. In April 1946 Lieutenant Colonel T.K. Mukerjee and Major Bhattacharjee were posted in as CO and Second-in-Command of 2 Signal Training Battalion. Soon afterwards, Captain K.K. Tewari was posted to the STC as the Adjutant and Major Tery Barreto as OC 'G' Company, which had led the mutiny.

Disciplinary action taken against those who participated in the mutiny was severe and swift. Those against whom there was even the slightest inkling were punished. Most of them were charged under Indian Army Act Section 27 (a)—"joining, exciting, causing or conspiring in a mutiny", and Army Act Section 27 (b)—"being present at a mutiny and not using his utmost endeavours to suppress the same". A total of 85 men were found to have been actively involved in the mutiny. Eighteen men were tried by Summary General Court Martial, of which 15 were sentenced to dismissal and imprisonment ranging from one to three years, with three being acquitted. Seven men were dismissed without trial and 19 discharged without terminal benefits. In addition, 41 were discharged from service on administrative grounds—services no longer required—without any enquiry or investigation. Many more were sent home merely on suspicion and the statements of Viceroy's and non-commissioned officers who were considered loyal by British officers. Most of these men had put in long years of service and fought in World War II. They did not get any pension or gratuity and many lived and died in penury. Their pleas for redress fell on deaf years as instructions were also issued not to entertain any petition or appeal unless Army Headquarters recommended it. Old records contain several letters that bring out the pathetic state of these unfortunate soldiers, who remained true to their salt and helped the British win World War II. Having implicit faith in the British sense of fair play and justice, they were surprised and disappointed at the treatment they received at the hands of the Government of the day.

Colonel (later Major General) R.J. Moberly was the last British officer to hold the appointment of Commandant, 1 Signal Training Centre, from 26 May to 1 December 1947. According to him, the mutiny need never have happened except for the following causes:[7]

> Standards of discipline and Military Training in Jubbulpore had been allowed to slip during the later war years. This was partly due to a high proportion of temporary British Officers with little experience of India. It was also partly due to a policy of retaining instructors for far too long. They became restless to see some active service, and the whole training machine lost touch with the requirements of the fighting units. Experienced senior officers were brought back into the training organization too late. After his return to Jubbulpore the writer discussed the trouble that had taken place in the Signal Training Centre with a number of senior Viceroy's Commissioned Officers some whom he had known before. They had known that trouble was brewing long before it actually happened. But their superiors did not consult them, and were out of touch with their men.

The men who refused to obey orders were in the Training Regiment responsible for the mechanic trades. Their accommodation was bad, their canteen almost non-existent, they never went on parade, having completed 'Military Training', and some were influenced by civilian members of the Records Office who lived in the city.

Though bad food and living conditions appeared to be the immediate causes of the mutiny at Jubbulpore, it had a political tinge right from the beginning. The firing on the naval ratings at Bombay and the punishments awarded to the officers of the Indian National Army were included in the list of grievances given by the mutineers on the first day itself. Throughout the revolt, the participants carried flags of the Congress and the Muslim League and shouted slogans such as 'Jai Hind' and 'Inquilab Zindabad'. On 27 and 28 February, they contacted local political leaders and sought their help. The local Congress leaders visited the mutineers under detention in the Jat lines and persuaded them to give up their resistance. They were shown a letter from Maulana Azad, the Congress President, asking them to resume work.[8]

During a press conference on 3 March 1946, Pandit Jawaharlal Nehru referred to the Jubbulpore mutiny, and said:

'... the men ... have remained completely peaceful...The demands were for better treatment in regard to rations, amenities etc. and equality of treatment between Indian and British soldiers. There were also some political demands ... Such demands should not normally be made on the basis of a strike... We have seen recently strikes by American and British servicemen'.[9]

Seth Govind Das of the Congress Party raised the matter in the Central Assembly in Delhi on 15 March 1946. In his reply, the War Secretary, Mr. Philip Mason gave the official version of the case. According to him, 1,716 persons were involved in the mutiny. He accepted that thirty-five persons had been wounded of whom eight had bayonet wounds with remainder having minor injuries from barbed wire or contusions. Only two persons were seriously injured and there were no deaths. However, he denied that there was any firing or bayonet charge. According to him, some persons had sustained bayonet wounds when they attempted to overpower the troops that had been called in to arrest the ringleaders. Mr. Ahmad Jaffar of the Muslim League suggested that a couple of members of the Defence Consultative Committee should be associated with the Inquiry, but this was rejected by the War Secretary, who contended that this was a service inquiry under the Indian Army Act, and it would be quite illegal to associate non-officials.[10]

A copy of letter written by Naik Soman on 28 February 1946 to his sister is reproduced below. This was probably censored en route but shows the feelings then prevalent amongst the soldiers in the Signal Training Centre:[11]

> Dear Sister,
>
> Your letter has been received. I and Babu both are quite well. Your message has been passed to him. Something dangerous is happening. Yesterday I together with 300 men went out with Congress Flag and the same has been started in every unit. Many have been arrested. Some were beaten with knives and some were wounded by firing—as a result some men have died and some are in bad condition. This process is still going on. We have also arranged to dishonour the British on the 6th of this month. We asked for the release from custody of our men but the reply was in negative. Everyone in India has started this—I don't know what troubles are bound to come to me. Whatever may happen I am willing to give my life. Indian sepoy has created the mutiny—you can ask God for blessing. For the help of British some troops have come to beat us. It is very dangerous but our blood is boiling. British are humiliating us let this become known to the World. We will arrange to get them out of India. Wherever I have been—Swaraj is discussed. We went out the other Castes have not helped us. But they cannot stop us. This is our last hurdle. I am very pleased that all is well at home. What you have said about Certificate reg your Babu—this could be done only after this victory.

Father, Mother, Kamla, Lilla—to all boys Kissing from us. Write. Write to Babu. Kissing from us to wife of brother.

There were similarities between the RIN Mutiny and the STC Mutiny. The grounds for both were similar—bad food, unhygienic living conditions, discrimination between British and Indian troops, ill-treatment by British officers, delay in demobilisation and resentment against the INA trials. Both mutinies were started by signallers, the one at Jubbulpore by personnel of the Signal Corps and the one at Bombay by personnel of HMIS *Talwar*, a shore establishment that trained wireless operators. Though they started on different dates, both mutinies finished on the same date, that is, 3 March 1946. However, where the two mutinies differed was in scale and the use of violence. The Jubbulpore mutiny was localised in a few units of the STC, and did not spread to other Army units located nearby. Starting from Bombay, the Naval mutiny embraced almost the entire naval fleet and spread to Karachi, Calcutta and several other naval stations. The Jubbulpore mutiny was characterised by non-violence. It was a passive demonstration by soldiers who only wanted their grievances to be heard. The ratings at Bombay resorted to widespread looting and damaged government property, the first target being the duty free canteen, which was ransacked of all imported goods, especially vast quantities of Scotch whisky. They also removed weapons from the armoury and opened fire, which had to be silenced by use of howitzers and mortars, resulting in several deaths. Several cars in the city were set on fire, and police officers were burnt alive.[12]

The mutiny in the Signal Training Centre and the Indian Signal Corps Depot and Records at Jubbulpore was the only major uprising in the Indian Army after the end of World War II. It was also the last uprising by soldiers under the British Raj. In a sense, it was the proverbial 'last straw' that broke the camel's back. Fearful of the effect it might have on the rest of the Army, news about the mutiny was deliberately suppressed. Having occurred in a small town, it was almost ignored by the national newspapers based in Delhi and Bombay. The Corps of Signals also chose to ignore the mutiny, even after Independence, and old timers talked about it only in hushed voices. Many officers were worried about the stigma associated with a mutiny, which has always been regarded as the most heinous of military offences. The fact that the Corps of Signals continued to be headed by a British officer up to 1954 may have played a part in this. Strangely enough, no record of the Jubbulpore mutiny exists in the National Archives or the Historical Section of the Ministry of Defence. As a result, it has been ignored by military historians as well as those who have written about the freedom struggle. The men involved in the mutiny have also suffered—unlike the participants in the Naval Mutiny, they have not been classified as freedom fighters. This is an injustice, considering that the ratings who took part in the Naval Mutiny resorted to violence, burning shops and buses; while the mutiny at Jubbulpore was peaceful, without any violence or damage to public property. Moreover, the mutiny at Jubbulpore was inspired by a sense of nationalism and political demands were included from the very beginning. The typewritten ultimatum issued by the Mutineers on 27 February 1946 contained the following six points:[13]

- Refuse to be treated as slaves in own land.
- English soldiers get better treatment and better pay.
- Demobilisation to be speeded up.
- Protest against firing in Bombay, Karachi and Calcutta.
- Protest against victory celebrations in face of food crisis.
- Demand release of all Indian National Army Officers including Abdul Rashid and Burhanuddin.

Notes
1. STC to GHQ (I), 27 November 1945, Signals Museum (SM), Jabalpur, 242-C, fol. 94.
2. GHQ (I) to Comdt. ISC Depot & Records, 21 February 1946, (SM), 242-C, fol. 92.
3. STC to Jubbulpore Area, 9 March 1946, (SM), 242-C, fol. 93.
4. STC to Jubbulpore Area, 27 February 1946, (SM), 242-C, fol. 134.
5. Appx. 'B' to STC to Jubbulpore Area, 8 March 1946, (SM), 242-C, fol. 95.
6. Richards to Boyd, Gelston and Anderson, 1 March 1946, (SM), 242-C, fol. 58.
7. Reminiscences of Major General R.J. Moberly, CB, OBE.
8. Dipak Kumar Das, *Revisiting Talwar* (Delhi, 1993), p. 294.
9. Lt Gen. S.L. Menezes, *Fidelity and Honour* (New Delhi, 1993), p. 404.

10. Statement of Mr. Philip Mason, ICS, War Secretary, in the Central Legislative Assembly on 15 March 1946.
11. From records kept in the Corps of Signals Museum, Jabalpur.
12. Major General Shahid Hamid, *Disastrous Twilight* (London, 1986), pp. 24-26.
13. Jubbulpore Area Signal No Q1019 dated 28 February to HQ Central Command, Agra.

6
The Indian National Army— A Brief History

Birth of the INA

The INA was formally created in December 1941 by Captain Mohan Singh of 1/14 Punjab Regiment and Major Fujiwara Iwaichi of the Japanese Army. Mohan Singh claims that after his capture by the Japanese in Malaya on 11 December 1941 he was inspired by a sudden burst of patriotic feeling that had lain dormant until that time. According to him, he was encouraged by Japanese propaganda that exhorted all Asian races to "kick out the white devils from the East", and thought that if he approached the Japanese to help him in starting a movement for India's independence, he would be able to attract a large number of soldiers. At that time, Mohan Singh felt that his force *"would provide India with a new weapon, an organized and patriotic army to back up the non-violent struggle being carried from within by the Indian National Congress."*[1]

In fact, the creation of the INA was part of a well-planned strategy evolved by Japan even before the commencement of the war in the Pacific. Indian nationalist movements had taken root in Thailand, Malaya, Burma and Sumatra, under the leadership of Baba Amar Singh and Sardar Pritam Singh. In Japan, Rash Behari Bose, Raja Mahendra Pratap and AM Sahay formed the nucleus of the Indian nationalist movement. Even before Japan entered the war, the Imperial General Headquarters in Tokyo sent Major Fujiwara Iwaichi to Bangkok to enlist the support of the Indian nationalist elements in South East Asia and induce the defection of Indian soldiers of the British Army, should war break out. An agreement was signed between Amar Singh and Colonel Tamura of the Japanese Army, according to which the Indian Independence League (IIL) agreed to collaborate with the Japanese by inciting and undermining the loyalty of the soldiers of the Indian Army. Leaflets in English, Gurmukhi and Hindustani were kept ready to be thrown among them exhorting them to disobey the orders of their English commanders if asked to fight against the Japanese.[2]

On 8 December 1941 the Japanese invaded Malaya. Captain Mohan Singh's battalion, 1/14 Punjab, was part of 15 Indian Infantry Brigade, then deployed near Jitra. After a preparatory bombardment with mortars, Japanese tanks attacked the position on 11 December 1941. The battalion literally disintegrated, with most of the personnel being captured immediately or during the course of the next few days, while trying to escape southwards towards Singapore. Mohan Singh was part of a group that included his CO, Lieutenant Colonel LV Fitzpatrick, who was wounded.[3]

On 15 December 1941 Mohan Singh's group met Major Fujiwara and Giani Pritam Singh, who had been following the Japanese as they advanced through Malaya. Pritam Singh and Fujiwara explained to Mohan Singh their plans for raising an army to fight for Indian independence. Mohan Singh was highly impressed with Fujiwara, who was a genuine idealist and a great believer in the concept of the Greater Asia Co-Prosperity Sphere. With arguments backed by phrases such as 'Asia for Asiatics' and India's 'shackles of slavery', Fujiwara convinced Mohan Singh that India was not going to be free by non-violent methods being advocated by Mahatma Gandhi. If Indians wanted freedom, they would have to fight for it. He told Mohan Singh, *"If you really want freedom for your country you must aspire to do something active. You must raise an Indian National Army."*[4]

After detailed discussions with Fujiwara, Mohan Singh agreed to raise the INA according to the model suggested by the Japanese. It soon became apparent that the role that the Japanese government was ready to allot to the INA was marginal. Instead of a fighting force, the Japanese intended to use the INA for propaganda purposes, particularly to foster anti-British feeling among Indian soldiers and the Indians in the region, for controlling prisoners of war and for maintaining law and order among the Indian population. Though Mohan Singh found Fujiwara to be a well-informed person, he felt that his knowledge of the strength and position of the Congress in India was poor. Whereas he had great regard for Mahatma Gandhi as a saint, he had not the slightest faith in his glorified weapon of non-violence. Mohan Singh tried to convince Fujiwara that under the prevailing conditions in India, the Congress method of fighting the British was the only practical one.[5]

It took less than 15 days for Mohan Singh to change his opinion about Mahatma Gandhi and the Congress, and fall in line with the stance of the Japanese. After discussions in Taiping on 30-31 December 1941, during which the Japanese handed over a memorandum on the role of the INA, Mohan Singh wrote to Fujiwara on 1 January 1942, agreeing to accept the leadership of Subhas Chandra Bose and modifying his views with regard to the Congress: *"The day Mr. Subhas Chandra Bose's name comes before us, we promise that if it suits our purpose we will openly condemn the Indian National Congress."*[6]

After the battle of the Shin River on 7 January 1942, three Indian infantry brigades were dispersed. Many Indian prisoners of war, after being subjected to intensive propaganda by Mohan Singh and his men, agreed to transfer their allegiance to the Japanese. Singapore fell on 15 February 1942, and a large number of Allied soldiers surrendered. Different figures have been given by historians about the total number of Allied prisoners, the number of Indian soldiers and the number that agreed to join the INA. According to Mohan Singh, 45,000 Indian soldiers were handed over by Lieutenant Colonel Hunt to Fujiwara at Farrer Park on 17 February 1942, who handed them over to Mohan Singh. However, Menezes gives the figure of Indian soldiers as 60,000, which is also the number mentioned by Cohen, relying on Winston Churchill's *History of the Second World War*. After Mohan Singh spoke to the assembled Indian prisoners at Farrer Park, most of them cheered enthusiastically. They were then sent to the Bidadari Camp, but the officers were separated from the men and not allowed to talk to the latter. During the next few days, the prisoners were asked to volunteer for the INA, with implied threats by the Japanese that the non-volunteers would be ill-treated, and the leaders in any non-cooperation would be shot.[7]

Estimates vary as to the actual numbers that joined the INA when it was formed. Mohan Singh writes that 42,000 men volunteered, while 13,000 remained non-volunteers. According to him, approximately one-third of the officers and one-fifth of the VCOs did not join. Gerard Corr writes that out of the 55,000-60,000 Indian prisoners, probably about 20,000 enlisted immediately.[8] Approximately the same figure is given by Joyce Lebra, who writes that close to 25,000 of the 45,000 Indians taken prisoner at Singapore did not volunteer.[9]

Mohan Singh promoted himself from captain to general, and became the GOC (General Officer Commanding) of the INA. He set about organising the newly formed Army, using novel techniques. All subedars and subedar majors were given the rank of captain, while jemadars were made lieutenants. To gain the confidence of these newly promoted officers, who were much older than the Indian Commissioned Officers (ICOs), Mohan Singh decided to give them command of battalions and brigades, using the ICOs to fill staff appointments such as brigade major, staff captain, adjutant, etc. The command of the brigade was given to Subedar Onkar Singh of 5/4 Punjab Regiment.

The first INA division was raised on 1 September 1942. Mohan Singh wanted to raise two divisions, but the Japanese agreed to only one. The division had three brigades, which were commanded by Lieutenant Colonels I.J. Kiani (Gandhi Brigade), Aziz Ahmed Khan (Nehru Brigade) and Prakash Chand (Azad Brigade). Lieutenant Colonel J.K.T. Bhonsle was given command of No. 1 Field Force Group, which had three infantry battalions and a heavy gun battalion. Lieutenant Colonel Burhanuddin commanded the Bahadur Group. The other functionaries were Major Jaswant Singh (Intelligence Group); Colonel M.S. Brar (Propaganda and Welfare Group), Lieutenant Colonel Kulwant Rai (Medical Group), Major S.A. Malik (Reinforcement Group), Lieutenant Colonel Shah Nawaz Khan (Officers Training School) and Major A.B. Mirza (HQ POWs).

Gradually, Mohan Singh began to realise that the Japanese had no intention of building up the INA into a strong military force. They wanted to use the INA more as a political pawn than a military weapon. In fact, the role that they had envisaged for the INA was propaganda, fifth column duties and minor military operations. They hoped that when they marched into India with the INA *"they would be acclaimed as liberators of India and Indians would automatically join them and the plum of victory will fall into their lap, ripened by the heat of their own activity. Thus they intended to use us as spies, euphemistically calling us patriots and freedom fighters."*[10]

Disillusioned by the Japanese attitude and his differences with Rash Behari Bose, the President of the IIL, Mohan Singh decided to dissolve the INA. On 21 December 1942 he signed a Special Order of the Day formally dissolving the INA. The Japanese promptly arrested Mohan Singh, and placed the INA under the IIL, headed by Rash Behari Bose, an Indian revolutionary who had married a Japanese and lived in Tokyo. He was under the influence of the Japanese and Mohan Singh had earlier refused to accept his authority over the INA, leading to differences between them. Though Mohan Singh had taken a pledge from his officers that the INA would not be raised again, this was soon forgotten. J.K.T. Bhonsle became the new Commander of the INA, with the title of Director, Military Bureau.

The Arrival of Subhas Chandra Bose

Subhas Chandra Bose was then in Germany, having reached there after his dramatic escape in January 1941 from Calcutta, where he had been placed under house arrest by the British authorities. With the support of the Germans, he had tried to raise the Indian Legion from the Indian prisoners of war in North Africa. However, he met with limited success, and only about 3,000 prisoners agreed to join him. It was only after a year that Bose was able to have an audience with Hitler, and request him to recognise his movement or at least announce that India would be granted independence after the war. Hitler felt that such a declaration was premature, and asked Bose to wait until German forces had advanced far enough. After German losses at Alamein and Stalingrad, it became clear that this would not happen. Bose then requested the Germans to arrange his move to South East Asia, where he had already been invited to take over the IIL and the INA. On 8 February 1943 Bose left Kiel in a German submarine, accompanied by Abid

Hasan. On 28 April 1943, he was transferred to a Japanese submarine near Madagascar, reaching Sabang in Northern Sumatra on 6 May and Tokyo on 16 May 1943. This was not the first, or indeed the last time that Bose left his followers to their fate, moving to greener pastures. In the words of Fay: *"Bose left behind three thousand Indian men in Wehrmacht uniforms whose future would be half-hearted participation in the manning of the Atlantic Wall and then a British prisoner of war cage—three thousand men and a wife and child."*[11]

On his arrival in Tokyo, Bose found the Japanese more accommodating than the Germans. Prime Minister Tojo received him soon after his arrival, and was quite receptive to his project of forming a provisional government in exile. On 16 June 1943 ,Tojo made a declaration in the Diet that Japan was firmly resolved to extend all help to India to achieve full independence. This was music to the ears of Bose, who had tried for almost two years to get a similar commitment from Hitler, without success. He made a series of radio broadcasts, publicising his presence in South Asia, calling Japan India's greatest friend. He received a tumultuous welcome when he reached Singapore on 2 July 1943, followed by week-long celebrations that were later commemorated annually as '*Netaji* Week'. On 4 July, he accepted the Presidency of the IIL and the allegiance of the INA, which he reviewed on the next day, giving it the battle cry '*Chalo Dilli*' (To Delhi). Two days later, another parade was held, at which Tojo himself took the salute.

On 8 August 1943, Subhas Chandra Bose assumed personal command of the INA. Unlike Mohan Singh, who had taken the rank of general, Bose held no military rank—he was just the Supreme Commander. However, he wore a uniform that was neither Indian nor British, but was similar to what he had seen in Italy and Germany—breeches, tunic and jack boots. (The only other member of the INA to wear breeches was Captain Lakshmi Swaminathan, who commanded the Rani of Jhansi Regiment.) The uniform was not the only thing Bose took from the Germans and Italians. Hitler and Mussolini had titles—Fuehrer and Il Duce—and deciding that he too must have one, he settled on '*Netaji*' (The Leader). On 21 October 1943, Bose announced the formation of the *Arzi Hukumat-e-Hind*, or the Provisional

Government of Free India, which was recognised by Japan, Germany, Italy and some other countries that were under Axis domination. A few days later, the Provisional Government declared war on Great Britain and the United States. Bose made the declaration of war at a rally of fifty thousand Indians, who were asked to ratify it, by standing up and raising their hands if they were prepared to lay down their lives. The audience rose instantly, cheering, raising their rifles in the air, and shouting, *"Netaji Ki Jai! Inqilab Zindabad! Chalo Delhi!"* The declaration proved to be a windfall for the new government—during the next few days over thirteen million dollars were collected from Indians in Singapore and Malaya. The money was spent as soon as it poured in.[12]

In November 1943, Bose was invited to Tokyo for the Greater East Asia Conference, which he attended as an observer. During his visit, he met Prime Minister Tojo and requested that Japan formally hand over to the Provisional Government of Free India the Andaman and Nicobar islands in the Bay of Bengal, which the Japanese had occupied in early 1942. This would give his government a measure of legitimacy, he reasoned. Tojo demurred, since the islands were strategically important, and the Japanese Navy was bound to object strongly. Finally, a compromise was reached. Tojo announced that Japan was ready to hand over the islands shortly, as the initial evidence of her readiness to help in India's struggle for independence. This was a declaration of intent, not a de facto transfer. The distinction was significant, for the next step—the actual transfer of administration—was never taken by the Japanese Government.[13]

Military Operations Conducted by the INA
From the day of its inception, Mohan Singh had been pressing for the INA to be sent to the front to take part in actual operations and wanted to raise two divisions. However, the Japanese agreed to only one. Mohan Singh soon realised that the Japanese were not serious about making the INA a strong force that could conduct regular military operations. After the 'dissolution' of the first INA in December 1942, its strength had dropped to 12,000. After the arrival of Subhas Chandra Bose, about 10,000 prisoners

agreed to join and it was decided to raise two more divisions. The first operational exposure of the INA was in a minor role in the Arakan, where it was employed in small detachments. This was followed by two operations in Imphal and on the Irrawaddy, for which Bose was able to convince the Japanese to allot specific sectors to the INA, instead of using it in penny packets. Bose repeatedly stressed that advance into India must be led by the INA, and *"the first drop of blood to be shed on Indian soil should be that of a member of the INA."*

In the Arakan offensive in February 1944, INA special groups comprising espionage and propaganda elements totalling about 250 men were part of the Japanese offensive against the 5th and 7th Indian Divisions. These men were organised in small parties that had mainly nuisance value, shouting propaganda or confusing orders in encounters with British-Indian troops, leading them sometimes into Japanese ambushes and spying out their defensive positions. One of these parties led by Major L.S. Misra managed to subvert an Indian outpost held by a platoon of Gwalior Lancers. This was touted as major success by the INA, Bose calling it an 'active and important' part in a great Japanese victory, which alas never materialised, the Arakan battle ending in a shattering defeat for the Japanese.[14]

The next operation in which the INA took part was the Japanese offensive against Imphal in March 1944. A group of about 150 irregulars of the INA Special Forces was attached to each of the three divisions that the Japanese employed in Imphal. The only regular INA division available was the 1st INA Division, under Colonel M.Z. Kiani—the 2nd Division was in Malaya—which comprised the 1st (Subhas) Regiment with a strength of 3,000 men, and the 2nd and 3rd Regiments, each two thousand strong. (The regiments were akin to brigades, and were sometimes referred to as such.) The first to be mobilised was the Subhas Regiment, under Lieutenant Colonel Shah Nawaz Khan, which was sent to the front with great fanfare, after a farewell speech by Bose himself on 3 February 1944. No. 1 Battalion, under Major P. S. Raturi was despatched to the Kaladan Valley, while No. 2 and 3 Battalions (Majors Ran Singh and Padam Singh) were to proceed to Haka and Falam area in the Chin Hills.

No. 1 Battalion reached the Kaladan Valley on 24 March as the 81st West African Division was withdrawing. It had several skirmishes with the rear guards, suffering a few casualties. It remained there intact, without further encounter, until September posting a company at Mowdok in the Sangu Valley, on Indian soil, during the monsoon. The crossing of the border was accompanied by great jubilation. According to the Japanese plan, Imphal was to be captured by 10 April 1944. The 2nd and 3rd Guerilla Regiments reached Rangoon only in March when the offensive was well underway and there was little chance of them playing a role in the battle. However, Bose had persuaded General Kawabe to let them at least enter Imphal on the heels of the Japanese. In any case, nobody expected that these men would have to fight. They were to line the route at Bose's entry into Imphal and assist in the formation of the new divisions there.[15]

The 2nd Guerilla Regiment (Lieutenant Colonel I.J. Kiani) together with the headquarters of the 1st INA Division commenced their move from Rangoon on 25 March. On his arrival at Maymyo on 28 March the Divisional Commander, Colonel M.Z. Kiani, was told that if he wished to be present at the fall of Imphal, he should immediately rush his force to Tamu and join the Yamamoto Force, which was part of the Japanese 33rd Division. 2nd Regiment moved post-haste, leaving behind all its heavy baggage, mortars and machine guns at Kalewa, with the men carrying only a blanket, a rifle and fifty rounds of ammunition. The Regiment reached the village of Khanjol towards the end of April and was informed that it would take part in the attack on Palel airfield, in conjunction with the Japanese thrust, which was planned for 1 May. With great difficulty the Regiment was able to muster 300 ex-Indian Army soldiers, who were grouped in a task force under the command of Major Pritam Singh, a staff officer at divisional headquarters who volunteered to lead the assault. The force left Khanjol on the night of 30 April but took almost two days to travel the twelve miles to the assembly area, reaching there on 2 May. The Japanese attack had gone in a day earlier from the East, but Pritam Singh decided to attack from the South on his own.

The attack was launched on the night of 2 May. At about 2230 hours the leading company, moving in extended order, ran into a platoon of 4/10 Gurkha Rifles, about five miles short of the objective. The INA soldiers had been assured that neither British nor Indian troops would fire on them, and were talking and smoking as they walked, with no semblance of discipline. The Gurkhas, forewarned of their approach, waited for them to reach a suitable position and then opened fire. The INA soldiers panicked and scattered, but Pritam Singh rallied some of them and approached again, this time more cautiously. He tried to parley with the Gurkhas, asking them not to fire. When this failed, the INA column attacked the platoon, but was beaten back. Pritam Singh launched seven attacks, before deciding to call it off. He ordered a withdrawal, sending a patrol to carry out reconnaissance for a new attack and calling his regimental commander for help. Two INA officers and many soldiers were killed; about thirty-five more surrendered or were captured. The Gurkhas lost two killed. Shortly afterwards the regimental headquarters was attacked by a company of the Frontier Force Rifles, followed by an air strike, in which fifty INA soldiers were killed and about the same number wounded. An artillery concentration severely shook the morale of the rest, and Kiani ordered the 2nd Regiment to withdraw to Khanjol. The reconnaissance patrol sent by Pritam Singh had also surrendered.[16]

The failure at Palel and the casualties were a severe jolt to the morale of the INA, which had come to believe the assurance given by Bose that propaganda and not firepower would decide the result when they faced Indian troops. Even for the Japanese, the battle was not going according to plan. By the first week of May the offensive of the Yamamoto Force had lost steam. The INA continued to hold Khanjol and Mittong Khunue in spite of frequent attacks and temporary withdrawals. Rains throughout May and June restricted activity on both sides to patrolling and the 2nd Guerilla Regiment did not fight any more battles. But the effects of climate, hunger and malaria took a heavy toll and by the beginning of July the strength of the Regiment was down to 750 men. On 3 July an Indian battalion, the 4th Mahratta Light Infantry, attacked and cleared Khanjol, which was held by just 50 men, and occupied Mittong Khunue. The Indian battalion did not advance further, and continued to hold the end of the Mombi track until it finally withdrew in the third week of July.

The 3rd Guerilla Regiment, under Lieutenant Colonel Gulzara Singh, did not play any significant part in the Imphal battle. The Regiment reached Tamu on 26 May after the monsoon had broken and was ordered to occupy a defensive position around Narum. One battalion was used for transport duties with the other two occupying the villages of Lamyang, Keipham and Khosat. The Regiment was already depleted by sickness when it arrived in the battle area. The rains and irregular supplies added to their woes, reducing the strength of the battalions to almost half. Both the 2nd and 3rd Guerilla Regiments and the remnants of the 1st Regiment began to withdraw on 18 July 1944.

Though the campaign ended in July by the end of April 1944 it had become clear that the offensive against Imphal was not going well. However, INA headquarters in Maymyo, without any means of communications with the forward troops, was unaware of this development, and in mid-May Bose sent three senior ministers of his cabinet—Chatterji, Alagappan and AM Sahay—to Tamu, partly in order that they might be at hand when Imphal was entered, and to buy up supplies, the INA difficulties and bring back an accurate report. Their report reached Bose towards the end of June but he was still unaware of the actual state of affairs. Even on 10 July when the Japanese officially informed Bose that the Imphal campaign was being abandoned, he appeared to have no inkling of the magnitude of the disaster. (No one has been able to explain the reason for lack of communications between Bose and his field commanders. There must have been hundreds of wireless sets in the equipment captured from the British at Singapore. Bose also had a secret radio link to Germany, on which he sometimes spoke to Nambiar, and also his wife.) Netaji Week was celebrated in Rangoon with customary gusto, including parades, speeches and cultural events. Bose issued a statement on the year's progress, and finalised the government organisation that would be needed once Imphal was captured. He broadcast messages to the people of India, including those who worked for the government, and to soldiers of the Indian Army, assuring them that they would be taken into the INA after victory, and their service would count towards their INA pensions!

The decision to suspend the Imphal campaign was made public on 26 July the day the Japanese Prime Minister Tojo resigned. It was only in August when survivors from the front began arriving in Rangoon with tales of horrible deaths due to disease and starvation that Bose was enlightened of the magnitude of the tragedy that had befallen his soldiers. On 19 August, there was a desperate appeal from Colonel Kiani to intervene with the Japanese to save hundreds of sick men stranded by floods on the withdrawal route. Bose was helpless, for the Japanese were themselves in dire straits and could do little to help the INA. Bose blamed the Japanese for the debacle, by denying essential supplies to the INA, and recommended the dissolution of the Hikari Kikan that had been responsible for this task. In future, the INA would look after all their administration themselves, he declared. He was enraged when he came to know of the large number of desertions in the INA and publicly berated the officers for their lack of leadership, which resulted in low morale of the troops. Of 6,000 men that had been sent to the front, at least 1,500 had deserted or been captured.

In October 1943, Bose received an invitation to visit Tokyo from the new Japanese Prime Minister, General Koiso. Bose found the Japanese still receptive to his demands, which included the appointment of an ambassador to his government, increase in the size of the INA by at least 50,000, a loan agreement, better weapons including tanks, planes and guns to supplement captured British stores, distribution of propaganda literature written by himself and transfer of all Indian POWs to the INA. At this time, American bombers were already paying frequent visits to the Japanese capital, and many of these demands appeared to be meaningless, which is probably the reason for the Japanese conceding them. However, in return for sending a diplomat to his government, the Japanese asked for a *quid pro quo*—Bose agreed to put the INA under Japanese command during the defence of Malaya and Burma.[17]

Though the writing was on the wall, Bose continued to exhibit his confidence that the Japanese would win the war. In an article in the *Azad Hind* on 6 November 1944, after the retreat from Imphal, he reiterated his firm conviction that the final victory would belong to Japan and Germany. *"A new phase of war was approaching"*, he wrote, *"in which the initiative would again lie in the hands of the Japanese."* Not surprisingly, Professor Joyce Lebra was constrained to write: *"Bose's constant repetition of this faith throughout and even after the Imphal campaign raises the question of the soundness of his military judgement."*[18]

After spending a month in Japan, Bose returned to Singapore in December 1944. He spent over a month in Malaya, reviewing the functioning of the training camps at Seletar and Kuala Lumpur, and going over the finances. On both counts he found the outlook dismal. The number of new recruits barely matched those who were shedding their uniforms and slipping away. The income of the Indian Independence League was drying up, and when persuasion failed, draconian measures were adopted to increase collections.

At a press conference in Rangoon the day after his arrival, Bose asserted that the war had now entered the third phase, which would be decisive, and Indians must play their rightful part. *"Had the rains not intervened"*, he said, *"we should by now have occupied the Manipur basin."* During a rally in October he had given a new war cry—*khun* (blood). In the days that followed, he repeated it at every opportunity. He no longer talked of the march to Delhi, but blood. It was Indian blood that he wanted, and he asked for it because the old slogan did not sound convincing now. The war was not over, but Bose knew that his men were not going anywhere near Delhi. Yet, the fight must go on. Freedom, he observed, carries a price—blood. And since blood was all that his young recruits had to offer, it became his constant refrain in the months that followed. *"Tum mujhe khun do, main tumhen azadi dunga"* (give me blood, and I will give you freedom), he said. As 1945 opened, this was all Bose had to offer.[19]

After their defeat at Imphal, Japanese forces had withdrawn to the Irrawaddy River, where the next major battle was to take place. Two INA divisions, the 1st and the 2nd, were to take part in the battle. In the event, only one regiment of the 2nd Division, the 4th Guerilla Regiment under Major G.S. Dhillon, could take part, the rest still waiting in Rangoon for their stores and equipment to arrive from Malaya. Mutiny and desertion had become a serious problem in the INA, and troops were screened before being sent to the front. About 150 men from Dhillon's regiment were sent back as suspect, leaving him with 1,200 men to defend twelve miles of the river. Bose ordered several measures to raise the morale of the troops. They were protected from contact with Imphal survivors and encouraged by glowing accounts of INA heroism in battle. Gallantry awards were presented and there were accelerated promotions, including four major generals, one of them being Shah Nawaz Khan, the newly appointed commander of the 2nd INA Division.

The 7th Indian Division began to cross the Irrawaddy on 14 February 1945 at Nyangu and Pagan, where the 4th INA Regiment was deployed. The attacking troops suffered some casualties from medium machine guns in the INA defences, but managed to cross the river. About a hundred men of the 7th INA Battalion under Lieutenant Hari Ram surrendered at Nyangu and one hundred and forty of the 9th INA Battalion under Lieutenant Chandra Bhan showed a white flag and laid down their arms at Pagan. Shah Nawaz has chosen to gloss over these surrenders, mentioning only the gallantry of the INA troops and the casualties they inflicted on the enemy. *"Our men having used up all their ammunition resorted to bayonet charges, but eventually most of the men of the 7th Battalion were overpowered and had to surrender"*.[20]

However, Bose was deeply pained when he heard of the surrenders, and wrote to Dhillon: *"I have heard with grief, pain and shame of the treachery shown by Lieutenant Hari Ram and others. I hope that the men of the 4th Regiment will wash away the blot on the INA with their blood."* Worried by the desertions, Bose wrote another letter to an officer of the INA Police at Mandalay, *"According to my information the men who recently deserted from Mandalay ... are still in the Mandalay area. These men must be arrested and sent down to Rangoon under escort. If you cannot arrest them, they must be shot at sight."*[21]

On 17 March 1945, there was another action at Taungzin where Dhillon's troops are said to have redeemed their reputation, according to INA accounts. A British motorised column attacked an INA company under the command of Second Lieutenant Gian Singh Bisht, in which the company lost about forty men, including the company commander. Shah Nawaz has described the action thus: *"In the name of India and Indian independence they charged the enemy trucks. The enemy immediately debussed and hand to hand fighting ensued which lasted for full two hours, but our heroes would not give in. Forty of them sacrificed their lives after inflicting heavier losses on the enemy. The enemy was so impressed by their determination that they beat a hurried retreat."*[22] A more down-to-earth version of the action has been given by Fay, who writes: *"Near Taungzin one day a company of his let itself be trapped in the open by light tanks, armoured cars and infantry in trucks, tried vainly to break out with the bayonet and lost several score men dead or captured. ... But Dhillon was also prone to heroics. When the publicity people at Rangoon heard about the Taungzin disaster, they transformed it into a sort of latter-day Charge of the Light Brigade, and Dhillon was pleased."*[23]

The next action occurred at Mount Popa on whose western slopes the 2nd INA Regiment under P.K. Sahgal was occupying defences. Headquarters 2nd INA Division was also at Popa, under its newly appointed commander, Major General Shah Nawaz Khan. In February Bose decided to visit Mount Popa himself, to get a first-hand account of the conditions there. His first visit to the front line had to be cut short because the enemy got there first. He was in Meiktila on 25 February when news came that British tanks had reached Mahling, just twenty miles away. When Shah Nawaz advised that they should turn back, Bose refused, saying *"England has not produced the bomb that can kill Subhas Chandra Bose."* However, reason finally prevailed over bravado, and he fled from Meiktila, accompanied by a very anxious Shah Nawaz in the only staff car that they had. Everyone was armed to the teeth and ready for the worst, Bose sitting with a loaded tommy gun across his lap with Shah Nawaz beside him, his personal physician next to the driver and the liaison officer on the running board. The scene is now a key element of the Bose legend.

Soon after his return to Rangoon, Bose received the shocking news that five staff officers of 2nd INA Division—four majors and one lieutenant—had walked across to the British lines. Soon afterwards, British aircraft dropped leaflets signed by one of them, advising others in the INA to surrender. The shameful desertions soon became a topic of conversation in every Rangoon household and the subject of laughter in every Japanese mess. Bose was rattled by the treachery, and said that he would take his own life if such a thing happened again. He announced the observance of a 'Traitors' Day' in each INA unit, when deserters would be publicly dishonoured. He issued two special orders, outlining a number of measures to deal with the problem. One of these specified that *"every member of the INA—officer, NCO or sepoy—will in future be entitled to arrest any other member of the INA, no matter what his rank may be, if he behaves in cowardly manner, or to shoot him if he acts in a treacherous manner."*[24]

Unfortunately, the desertions did not stop. Late in March one of Dhillon's battalion commanders deserted. On the night of 2 April just before a full-scale attack on the 2nd INA Regiment at Legyi, three staff officers and some NCOs deserted. The attack came at midday and the INA defences soon collapsed, even the administrative area being overrun. Sahgal ordered a counterattack but the two platoons concerned deserted. A second counterattack after nightfall succeeded, but Sahgal then came to know that the whole of his 1st Battalion—the CO, company commander and about three hundred men—had deserted. The remainder could not face another attack and Sahgal withdrew them on his own initiative during the night. What followed was a rout. Except for an odd occasion when they decided to stand and fight, the 2nd INA Division disintegrated and virtually ceased to exist. By the end of April only fugitives remained at large. On 13 May 1945, Shah Nawaz, Dhillon and about fifty men surrendered at Pegu.

The End of the INA
Rangoon fell to British forces on 4 May 1945. A day earlier, the senior British officer who was a prisoner in the Rangoon jail had ordered the disarming and concentration of the INA, which was now under the command of

Major General Loganadhan, the Supreme Commander having left about ten days earlier along with a few senior officers, about fifty League workers and the last contingent of women of the Rani of Jhansi regiment. In his last message before leaving Bose declared *"I do not leave Burma of my own free will. I would have preferred to stay on here with you and share with you the sorrow of temporary defeat."* But his advisers had overruled him, he had other responsibilities in Siam and Malaya that nobody else could fulfil, and for Indians this defeat was only an incident in their struggle. *"Go down as heroes"*, he said, *"go down upholding the highest code of honour and discipline."*[25]

Bose's last words to his men were to "uphold the highest code of honour", which he was even then violating, perhaps unknowingly. Not being a professional soldier, he can be forgiven for not being aware of the time-honoured code that a captain always goes down with his ship and a commander with his troops, be it death or captivity. (Percival surrendered with 85,000 of his men when Singapore fell in 1942 and Niazi with 93,000 troops in 1971 in East Pakistan. Captain Mulla went down with the INS *Khukri* in 1971.) However, most of the senior INA officers had spent long years in uniform, and it appears strange that they advised him to escape, leaving more than ten thousand of his men to their fate.

It has been suggested that Bose wanted to go to Russia and carry on the struggle from there, but there appears no concrete proof of this. Another reason put forward is that the British authorities would have executed him if he had been captured, but this appears unlikely. Bose was never a member of the Indian Army and could not have been tried for treason under the Indian Army Act, like Shah Nawaz, Sahgal and Dhillon. His stature and prestige in India would have deterred the British from even contemplating such a step. In fact, the wave of sympathy that swept the country after the INA trials would have multiplied manifold and united the Indian people against the British. Who knows, with Bose being present at the final parleys, India may not been partitioned.

The INA ceased to exist after its remnants surrendered to British forces on 4 May 1945. The Supreme Leader of the INA, Netaji Subhas Chandra Bose died in a plane crash shortly after this. But the legend of Bose refuses to die. Anton Pelinka has a very interesting and plausible reason for this 'mythos' as he calls it. He writes:

> Whatever Bose had in mind when his plane crashed on August 18, 1945, he could no longer realize it. But in the imaginations of millions of people in India (and likely also in Pakistan and Bangladesh), Bose lived on. Above all, there remained the fact that independence did not come to mean a high standard of living for the many but rather expulsion and death for millions and the still unsolved problem of mass poverty. In the face of all these disappointments, Bose embodied the hope that remained unfulfilled.

> And for that reason, he was not allowed to die. The Bose mythos begins with the doubt that Subhas Chandra Bose actually perished in the plane crash of August 18, 1945 in Taipei. Many people were willing to believe in a cover-up of mass proportions, regardless of who might have carried it out. Bose was alive, it was said, or had been seen somewhere, he was alive in a Soviet camp, he was a high ranking member of Mao's People's Liberation Army and would soon, very soon, in fact, return to India. He would come, like a messiah, to eradicate all evil and thus, to fulfill the unfulfilled promises of independent India. (Bose, M., 1982, p. 251)

Numerous commissions of the Indian government have examined the circumstances surrounding his death. They all arrive at the same conclusion: Bose died on August 18, 1945 in Taipei from severe burns sustained in the plane crash. Bose's family also subscribes to this interpretation (Bose, Sisir, interview, 1999; Bose, Sugata, interview, 2001). But the legend refuses to die. The hundredth anniversary of his birth was celebrated intensively in India, particularly in Calcutta. The city administration in Calcutta, the Calcutta Municipal Corporation, published a detailed report on Bose's life works. In this special edition of the Calcutta Municipal Gazette, Bose's death is reported in lapidary fashion: "The mysteries concerning his death remain unsolved till date". (Calcutta Municipal Gazette 1997: 344)

The fact that Calcutta was and continues to be the place where Bose's mythos is cultivated points to a further function of this mythos. Bose stands for Bengal's disappointments. Around 1900, Bengal was the most important part of British India, and Calcutta was the capital of the empire's crown jewel. But then Bengal lost more and more of its importance. The British moved the capital to Delhi, and Bengal seldom played an important role in the Indian National Congress. Bose was the exception to this rule. And then came the partition. After Punjab, Bengal was the second of India's traditional regions to be divided, with all of the terrible consequences for both sides.

Bose is the protest against the loss of significance, especially for the Bengali sense of self, against the dominance of Delhi, and that of Uttar Pradesh, against the predominance of Hindi. For Bengal, Bose could not be allowed to die. In the ongoing memory of him, Bengal celebrated self-pity and nostalgia (Chaudhuri 1987: 799). Bose's mythos is also Bengal's attempt to demand recognition of its importance within India.[26]

Notes

1. Maj. Gen. Mohan Singh, *Soldiers' Contribution to Indian Independence* (New Delhi: Army Educational Stores, 1974), p. 67.
2. T. R. Sareen, *Japan and the Indian National Army*, Agam Prakashan, 1986, pp. 51-52.
3. Joyce C. Lebra, *Jungle Alliance—Japan and the Indian National Army*, pp. 16-18. (Lebra erroneously writes that Mohan Singh was the second-in-command of the battalion. In fact, there were several officers senior to him, including Major VDW Anderson, the 2ic.)
4. Hugh Toye, *The Springing Tiger*, London, Cassell Publishers, 1959, p. 3.
5. Mohan Singh, p. 78.
6. Mohan Singh, p. 86.
7. Lt Gen S.L. Menezes, *Fidelity and Honour—The Indian Army from the Seventeenth to the Twenty-First Century*, New Delhi, Penguin, 1993, p. 382.
8. Gerard H. Corr, *The War of the Springing Tigers*, London, Osprey Publishing House, 1975, p. 116.
9. Lebra, p. 83.
10. Mohan Singh, p. 201.
11. Peter Ward Fay, *The Forgotten Army*, University of Michigan Press, 1993, p. 200.

12. Lebra, p. 130; M. Sivaram, *The Road to Delhi*, Institute of Southeast Asian Studies, 2012, p. 158.
13. Lebra, p. 133.
14. Toye, p. 105.
15. Toye, p. 106.
16. Toye, p. 226.
17. Lebra, p. 143; Sivaram, p. 230.
18. Lebra, p. 191.
19. Fay, p. 315.
20. Maj Gen Shah Nawaz Khan, *My Memories of INA and Its Netaji*, Delhi, Rajkamal Publications, 1946, p. 190.
21. Toye, p. 139.
22. Shah Nawaz, p. 195.
23. Fay, pp. 342-43.
24. Toye, p. 142, *Special Order of the Day*, 13 March 1945.
25. Toye, p. 146.
26. Anton Pelinka, *Democracy Indian Style—Subhas Chandra Bose and the Creation of India's Political Culture* (Routledge, 2003), pp. 8-9.

7
Subhas Bose & The INA—Some Unanswered Questions

The Indian National Army remains an enigma, even today. Throughout its life span of three years, and even later, the INA has generated several controversies and given rise to conundrums some of which remain unsolved. Ironically, during its existence the activities of the INA remained shrouded in mystery and it was only after it ceased to exist that most of these controversies surfaced. Though there is a wealth of literature available about the INA and its leader, Netaji Subhas Chandra Bose, many questions still remain unanswered. These are often discussed at debates and seminars and provide the topic for articles and books. Some of these questions will be discussed in this chapter.

Q1. Why Did Some Indian Soldiers Join the INA While Others Did Not?

In the Foreword to Toye's book, Philip Mason, who was the Joint Secretary in the War Department in 1945-1946, gives four motives for joining the INA. A few did so with the intention of rejoining British forces when they saw a chance; some were puzzled, misinformed, misled, and on the whole believed the course they took was the most honourable open to them; others were frankly opportunist and some really were fervent nationalists.

Stephen Cohen has given a similar analysis. *"At least three factors influenced the decision to join the INA: personal comfort, nationalist political beliefs, and the charismatic appeal of Subhas Bose. A few of the defecting officers anticipated personal rewards for themselves when they transferred allegiance* to the Japanese, and to this extent the British label of 'treasonous rabble' was accurate. No INA officer has ever admitted such a motive, but interviews with former INA leaders and British officers indicate that money and security were important considerations for a few Indians."[1]

Major (later Major General) Shahid Hamid was the Private Secretary to Field Marshal Sir Claude Auchinleck, the Commander-in-Chief in India in 1946-1947. According to him, *"Most of the men who joined the INA were cowards and were not prepared to face the hardships of the prisoner of war camps. It was an escape from ill treatment and starvation. Very few joined for patriotic reasons."*[2]

Some of the reasons given by ex-INA officers for joining the INA are interesting, even amusing. A number of officers such as Shah Nawaz, J.K.T. Bhonsle, Gian Chand, etc., did not join the INA initially, but later changed their minds. Shah Nawaz writes: *"We decided that the best course was (a) for the senior officers to join the INA, gain control of it and prevent the ill treatment of prisoners of war, and also their exploitation by the Japanese. If we were unable to do this, then we would try and wreck the INA from within, if and when we had an opportunity to do so. (b) For the rank and file to remain out of the INA and if need be to undergo hardships and ill treatment, but the senior officers in the INA would do their best to help them. This at that time concerned mainly the Muslims"*.[3]

The concern of Shah Nawaz for Muslims was one of the reasons that prompted his decision to join the INA. This has been confirmed by Harbaksh Singh, who writes that Shah Nawaz joined the INA *"because of some dispute over accommodation for a Muslim JQ"*. As for Bhonsle, Harbaksh does not mince words. *"Bhonsle, I knew, had done it to save his skin. He had admitted as much to me."*[4]

Prominent among those who did not join were Captain (later Lieutenant General) Harbaksh Singh, 5/11 Sikhs; Captain (later Major General) H.C. Badhwar; Captain (later Lieutenant General) KP Dhargalkar, both of the 3rd Cavalry and Captain (later Lieutenant General) A.C. Iyappa, Signals. The reasons for these officers deciding against joining the INA were mainly two—distrust of the Japanese and lack of faith in the INA leadership.

According to Harbaksh, *"unless Mahatma Gandhi or Pandit Jawahar Lal Nehru made an appeal over the air for every young man outside India to join the INA to liberate India with the help of the Japanese, we would not join, as we had no faith in its leadership"*.[5]

Cohen cites another reason for the professional soldier being less than sympathetic to the INA—his oath of loyalty. Many did not regard lightly the breaking of their oath, and preferred to spend the war in a prison camp undergoing privations at the hands of the Japanese or the INA. In India, the concept of loyalty is closely linked to 'salt'. An employee is expected to be loyal to his employer, whose salt he has eaten. For many Indian soldiers joining the INA meant being untrue to their salt, and facing the stigma of faithlessness and disloyalty in their regiments and villages when they returned home.

There is no doubt that those who refused to join faced hardships, hard labour, and even torture, sometimes by their own men. Some of the officers who refused to join were subjected to third-degree methods to bring them in line. Badhwar and Dhargalkar were locked in underground cages, which were about five feet long by five feet wide and seven feet high, and sometimes held five or six prisoners. They were kept inside these cages for 88 days, during which time they saw nothing of the outside world.[6]

The fate of those who refused to join the INA was uncertain. The fortunate ones remained in POW camps or were sent as working parties to depots and airfields. Many were sent to labour camps in Borneo, the Celebes and Thailand, where thousands died of disease and starvation. Those who joined the INA not only had a more comfortable life but also a better survival rate. According to Menezes, of the 40,000 prisoners of war who did not join the INA, 11,000 died in captivity, of disease, starvation or were murdered, some even cannibalised by the Japanese. Strangely enough, the Provisional Government of *Azad Hind*, which claimed the allegiance of all Indians and guaranteed equal rights and equal opportunities to all its citizens, did nothing to alleviate the sufferings of these unfortunate soldiers. Corr writes: *"As for Gill, suffering in solitary confinement, he (Bose) did nothing. Neither did he do anything for the thousands of Indians in Thailand* who were being worked to death on the Infamous Death Railway. He left them to their appalling fate."⁷

What is the truth? Did the majority of prisoners join the INA for patriotic reasons, or for pecuniary gains, better living conditions and to escape torture and harsh treatment at the hands of their Japanese captors?

Q2. Were the Aims of the INA Practical and Achievable?

In mid-January 1942 Mohan Singh said that the eventual object of the INA was to drive the British out of India. During the Bangkok Conference held in June 1942, the Indian Independence League resolved that the INA would be used for operations against British forces; to secure and safeguard Indian National Independence and for any other purpose that may assist the Independence of India. Soon after his arrival in South East Asia, Bose declared: *"Indians outside India, particularly Indians in East Asia, are going to organise a fighting force which will be powerful enough to attack the British Army in India. When we do so, a revolution will break out, not only among the civil population at home, but also among the Indian Army, which is now standing under the British flag."*⁸

The aim of the INA, as envisaged by Mohan Singh, the IIL and also by Bose was twofold—to militarily defeat the British and to subvert the loyalty of the Indian Army. Were these aims achievable? Bose was confident that as soon as he entered India, Indian soldiers would lay down their arms. However, it was the height of military naiveté to believe that the ill-trained and ill-equipped INA would be able to defeat the British Army. Mohan Singh, Shah Nawaz as well as several others have written that the Japanese did not support them with weapons, ammunition and supplies. If this was true, why did they agree to send their men into battle, where they were bound to suffer heavy casualties?

Though Bose was not a professional soldier, even he must have known that the military objectives of the INA were not achievable. According to Corr, Bose made two fatal errors of judgement during his career. The first was his decision to challenge Gandhi, which set him on the road out of India. The second error was to believe that he could return through military means. *"Bose was aware that the tide of war had turned against Japan and the Imphal offensive was a gigantic gamble. Yet he spoke to his men in a way that suggested the road to Delhi lay open. ... Becoming a victim of his own propaganda, Bose urged on his regiments to destruction. In the end he lost touch with reality."*[9]

After the defeat at Imphal, when General Kawabe told him that the order to retreat had been given, Bose declared that the INA would continue the operations. *"Increase in casualties, cessation of supplies, and famine are not reason enough to stop marching. Even if the whole army becomes only spirit we will not stop advancing towards our homeland. This is the spirit of our revolutionary army"*, he said. Though Corr writes that Kawabe was much moved, he must also have been amused at Bose's innocence. *"Prodigal with emotional language, Bose did not seem to feel he had been sufficiently prodigal with the lives of his soldiers. He talked—to the amazement of even the Japanese—of sending the Rani of Jhansi Regiment up to the battle front."*[10]

Having known that the INA did not have the military strength to defeat the British Army, why did its leaders send it into battle, to face death and destruction?

Q3. How Did the INA Perform in Battle?

Almost all ex-INA officers eulogise the gallantry of its members during operations. Some even suggest that the INA planned and executed the attack on Imphal, with the Japanese playing a subsidiary role. Shah Nawaz writes: *"While the INA was on the offensive there was not a single occasion on which our forces were defeated on the battle-field, and there was never an occasion when the enemy despite their overwhelming superiority in men and material were able to capture a post held by the INA. On the other hand there were very few cases where INA attacked British posts and failed to capture them."*[11]

According to Dr. R.M. Kasliwal, who was the personal physician to Bose in 1945, *"In the fighting in the Imphal sector our troops played a very prominent part. They pushed the enemy back everywhere ... Our armies, along with those of our allies chased the British forces deep into Manipur sector. Some of our troops reached Kohima and occupied that town, and some penetrated up to Dimapur."*[12]

The war diaries of the Indian Army formations and units that fought in Imphal not only contradict the INA claims but also contain unflattering accounts of their performance, which are endorsed by the Japanese who were fighting alongside. The low casualty figures and the large numbers of INA personnel who surrendered and deserted are also indicative of the pedestrian performance of the INA. Several foreign writers have commented on the performance of the INA in battle. Cohen writes: *"... the INA was starved of equipment, logistic support and information, and although it did occupy Indian soil briefly, its battle history was dismal."*[13] John Connell writes: *"In every recorded clash between British and Indian forces and the INA in Burma, the INA was worsted. Their leadership was far from inspiring: three officers in all were killed in battle, one was killed by a Japanese sentry and one died in an air crash."*[14]

One of the reasons for the INA's poor performance was the quality of its leaders. Commenting on this aspect, Toye writes: *"... few of the platoon and company commanders in the 1st INA Division had been trained as officers at all: most of them had been promoted direct from the ranks by Mohan Singh ... What quality of leadership could be expected of officers such as these in the war of 1944?"*[15]

In military terms, are the claims of INA victories genuine?

Q4. How Many INA Soldiers Were Killed in Battle?
Apart from their performance in battle, INA veterans make tall claims about the number of soldiers who died in battle. Captain S.S. Yadav, an ex-INA officer has compiled a book (*Forgotten Warriors*), listing the names of all members of the INA. This is also claimed to be the official history of the INA. The list contains about 13,000 names, with several appearing more than once and many addresses missing or incomplete. It has a list of 131 persons who died in action and a Roll of Honour listing the names of 1,602 persons who died from all causes, including wounds, sickness, accidents, etc. Yet, he writes: *"The valiant troops of the INA had to withdraw to Burma from the battlefronts of Kohima and Imphal. About twenty six thousand heroes of the Indian National Army laid down their lives."*[16] Shah Nawaz is more

conservative, stating that 4,000 INA soldiers were killed in the fighting in April and May 1944.

The INA figures appear to be grossly inflated. Quoting official figures given by GHQ India, Toye writes: *"The INA Division had started out for Imphal six thousand strong: only two thousand six hundred returned, and of these about two thousand had to be sent at once to hospital. During the campaign 715 men deserted, about four hundred were killed in battle, about eight hundred surrendered, and about fifteen hundred died of disease and starvation.*[17]

In subsequent operations, the number of desertions increased, while fewer were killed in action. Menezes writes: *"Of some 15,500 INA personnel in Burma in 1945, 150 were killed in action; 1,500 died of starvation or disease; 5,000 surrendered or deserted; 7,000 were captured; 2,000 escaped towards Bangkok.*[18]

It is obvious that the number of INA soldiers killed in action was much less than what is claimed in the official history. Unfortunately, there is no Roll of Honour or a war memorial on which the names of these fallen soldiers can be inscribed.

Q5. Were Indian Soldiers in the pre-Independence Indian Army Patriots or Mercenaries?

The soldiers of the INA fought against their compatriots in the British Indian Army. The professed aim of the INA was to free India from British rule. Hence they considered themselves as patriots and the Indians serving in the British Indian Army as mercenaries. This question had baffled most Indians of that time and does so even today.

Almost all officers who joined the INA claim that they did so for patriotic reasons. Of course, none of them has been able to explain why his sense of patriotism surfaced only after being captured. If they felt so strongly about serving under the British, they should have resigned. In the Preface to Toye's book, Philip Mason wrote, *"One must respect such a man as Subhas Chandra Bose, who resigned from the Indian Civil Service because he sincerely believed it his duty to India; that respect can hardly be extended to all who changed sides in adversity and who a second time chose the more comfortable path."*[19]

Mohan Singh feels differently, writing: *"In whatever dignified colours we may paint the pre-Independence Indian Army, we cannot hide one hard fact that, besides its responsibility for the defence and security of our country, it had to play its purely mercenary role."*[20]

Of course, there is an inherent contradiction in Mohan Singh's statement—responsibility for defence of one's country does not blend with a mercenary role. The primary task of the Indian Army, even under British rule, was defence and internal security of the country. In 1933 the War Office had spelt out the role of the Indian Army in the following words: *"The duties of the army in India include the preservation of internal security in India, the covering of the lines of internal communication, and the protection of India against external attack. Though the scale of forces is not calculated to meet external attack by a great Power, their duties might well comprise the initial resistance to such an attack pending the arrival of imperial reinforcements."*[21]

The supplementary role implied the provision of an Imperial Reserve, for which the British Government agreed to grant an annual subsidy of 1.5 million pounds to the Government of India. This role was modified by the '1938 Plan' (Document No. B-43746), which stipulated six tasks for the Indian defence forces, namely, defence of the Western Frontier against external aggression; defence of land frontiers other than the Western Frontier; maintenance of law and order and the suppression of disorder and rebellion; safeguarding strategic lines of communication within India; provision of a general reserve with mobile components; and provision of forces for possible employment overseas at the request of the Government of UK. In view of the enhancement in the responsibilities assigned to India, the Chatfield Committee was constituted in 1938 to recommend measures to modernise and increase the size of the Indian armed forces. The Committee recommended that a new contract be negotiated with the Government of India, to enable it to fulfil its task. The recommendations of the Committee were approved by the British Cabinet on 28 June 1939, but before they could be implemented, World War II broke out.

As will be obvious, the primary responsibility of the Indian Army—defence of India—never changed. The employment of Indian troops overseas was covered by a formal contract between the governments of UK and India. By definition, a mercenary soldier fights for money or reward for a country other than his own. Strictly speaking, the term would be more appropriate for the INA soldiers who fought for a foreign power—Japan. It is pertinent that the salaries of all ex-Indian Army soldiers in the INA were paid by Japan, the Provisional Government of *Azad Hind* paying only for the civilian recruits.

Who were the mercenaries—Indian soldiers in the Indian Army or the Indian National Army?

Q6. What Is the Truth about Atrocities Committed by the INA?

There were several reported instances of the INA soldiers committing atrocities on Indian soldiers who were captured and held in their custody, as well as on those who refused to join the INA. After the end of the war, some of them were tried by court martial and convicted, not only for waging war against the Crown but also murder, and causing grievous hurt. Of the three officers (Shah Nawaz Khan, P.K. Sahgal and G.S. Dhillon), who were tried in the Red Fort in 1945, Dhillon was charged with the murder of Duli Chand, Hari Singh, Daryao Singh and Dharam Singh, whereas the other two were charged with abetment to murder, in addition to waging war against the King. Later, Captain Burhanuddin was also tried for murder but found guilty only of causing grievous hurt. Apparently, *"Teja Singh was stood on a table, his wrists tied to a rope eight feet from the ground, the table removed, and Teja Singh beaten by 120 men in succession under Burhanuddin's orders until he lost consciousness, with the result that he subsequently died."*[22]

Commenting on the atrocities committed by the INA, Shahid Hamid writes: *"Most officers later realized that the INA was a trap, but once in they could not get out. They had no love for the Japanese and maintained that they were let down by them. The atrocities committed by the Kempatai (Japanese Special Military Police) did not help towards better relations. Taking their clue (sic) from the Kempatai the INA committed atrocious crimes in the name of patriotism against their own comrades. These are considered among the most degrading crimes in the history of soldiering."*[23]

However, there is a contrary view, which holds that stories of INA atrocities were sometimes concocted or deliberately exaggerated by British Intelligence, in order to protect Indian soldiers from falling prey to INA propaganda. According to Peter Ward Fay, in 1943 the British authorities adopted a programme that was intended to blacken the name of the INA, which was christened the JIFC (Japanese Indian or Inspired Fifth Column), which came to be known as Jiffs. Each unit was asked to form a 'josh group', in which officers were detailed to educate and train in countering INA propaganda and possible seduction by contact parties of the INA as had occurred in the Arakan. Interrogation files were combed for instances of barbarous behaviour by the Japanese towards prisoners, and these were circulated among troops deployed on the Burma Front. *"There is a purpose here. It is to instil hatred of the Japanese, contempt for traitors, and in general a desire to be 'up and at them' into the men".*[24]

The INA executed some of its own members, who were accused of desertion. This was done after trials conducted by the INA under its own Act, whose legality was suspect. However, Bose had himself decreed that traitors would be executed, even though he had earlier announced that anyone who wished to leave the INA could do so at any stage. There was the well-known case of Captain Durrani, who not only instructed several intelligence agents sent to India to surrender, but gave them intelligence to pass on to authorities in India. At a secret midnight arraignment in the Bidadri Concentration Camp, Bose personally interrogated Durrani, who was weak and dazed after ten days of Japanese third degree. Bose would take no denial. *"You should be grateful to me"*, he said, *"that I have saved you from the Japanese firing squad, and that you will be shot by Indians."*[25]

Q7. Did the INA Resort to Coercion to Collect Funds?

Maintaining a large military force like the INA needed considerable amount of funds. The Japanese agreed to pay the salaries of the prisoners of war, and to supply the weapons, equipment and rations. Most of the weapons and equipment were captured from the British Army after the fall of Singapore, and as it retreated from Burma. However, the civilian recruits had to be paid by the IIL, which had to rely on contributions from the Indian community in South East Asia. In the initial period these contributions were voluntary, and sufficed to meet the needs of the INA. However, after the arrival of Bose, the IIL was expanded, with a secretariat and eight departments to handle its multifarious activities. By October 1943 the monthly expenses amounted to about a million local dollars or 116,700 pounds sterling.

The arrival of Bose infused new life into the movement, and Indians made generous contributions. A merchant named Habeeb donated his entire estate to the IIL. Even poor Indians did not lag behind and gave whatever they could afford. However, the contributions soon dried up and persuasion was replaced by threats. On 25 October 1943, Bose addressed the merchants of Malaya with severity: *"Legally speaking there is no private property when a country is in a state of war. If you think that your wealth and possessions are your own, you are living in delusion. Your lives and property do not belong to you; they now belong to India and India alone."*[26]

When Bose heard that some of the rich Indians of Malaya were murmuring that he was harassing them, and wanted to change their nationalities or avoid payment by some other means, he told them; *"I stand here today representing the Provisional Government of Azad Hind which has absolute rights over your lives and properties ... If you do not choose to come forward voluntarily, then we are not going to remain slaves on that account ... Everyone who refuses to help our cause is ... our enemy."*[27]

Bose soon recognised that cash donations would not be enough to meet his needs and decided that he must make a systematic levy on Indian property. From the beginning of 1944 Indians had to declare their assets. Levies of from 10 to 25 per cent were imposed and collected with progressive vigour. After a state reception in Manila, Bose visited Saigon on 24 November 1943, where the Indian community was assembled to greet him. He assessed its contribution to his funds at twelve million *piastres* and, when the leaders demurred, exclaimed, much as he had done in Malaya: *"All your wealth would not buy back one life lost in battle. I have full jurisdiction over you and can order you to the front."*[28]

The shortage of funds was aggravated once it became clear that Japan was losing the war. In November 1944 the collection in Malaya fell from $2,000,000 to $617,000, in six months. It became difficult to enforce assessments—now that people knew that time was on their side, they delayed payments and concealed assets. In December 1944, Bose toured the region, to collect funds. In Penang he ordered the arrest of a defaulter, which had a salutary effect on the others. On his return to Singapore, he threatened ten people with arrest. Letters were sent out to each defaulter, with a warning that if they did not pay up within three days, they would face arrest and imprisonment. On his way back to Rangoon in January 1945 Bose addressed a public meeting. His speech was direct and bitter: those who opposed him should say so openly, they could then be put into concentration camps with the British and their property could be confiscated: if they wished to remain free they must pay their assessments. Bose left with the Japanese Security Police a list of ten persons for immediate arrest, and eighty others for varying degrees of surveillance and pressure: in the following two weeks the ten were arrested.[29]

In July 1945, 'Netaji Week' was celebrated in Singapore. The rich Indians were called for a meeting to hear new demands for money. On the orders of Bose, five of the defaulters warned in January were arrested by the Japanese Security Police. Several demand notes went out from the IIL. A man who had promised ten thousand dollars but sent only half received a terse note: *"I regret that our instructions are not to accept part payments. Netaji made it very clear that promises must be fulfilled in a day or two. It is incumbent on you to pay your promised amount at once."* Kuala Lumpur was similarly visited, where five defaulters were arrested.[30]

Were these coercive methods to extort funds from Indians living in foreign countries lawful?

Q8. What Is the Truth about Bose's Marriage to Emilie Schenkel and the Reasons behind Keeping It Hidden?

One subject that remains somewhat of a mystery is Bose's secret marriage to Emilie Schenkl, an Austrian girl he first met during his visit to Europe in the 1930s. She worked as his secretary and helped him produce *The Indian Struggle* in 1934. During a subsequent visit in 1937, she accompanied Bose to the health resort of Bad Gastein, where he wrote his autobiography, *The Indian Pilgrim*, which was published ten years later.[31]

Emilie was his secretary again in 1941, when he went to Germany after his dramatic escape from Calcutta and established the Free India Centre. Toye writes: *"In July 1942 it became necessary for Fraulein Schenkl, who had been Bose' private secretary for more than a year, to leave the Free India Centre. The dismissal was not what it seemed. Bose had known Emilie Schenkl ever since 1934; she was now secretly his wife, and in September 1942 was to bear him a daughter".*[32]

Though it is fairly certain Bose married Emilie Schenkl secretly in 1937 and they had a daughter named Anita Bose Pfaff in 1942, some questions about the marriage remain. It has not been clearly established if there was an actual marriage ceremony. Bose chose to keep his marriage a secret and did not reveal it except to a chosen few. What could be the reason for this? Several historians have written about it including members of his own family, such as Sugata Bose. He writes:

> On 4 November 1937, Subhas sent a letter to Emilie in German, saying that he would probably travel to Europe in the middle of November. "Please write to Kurhaus Hochland, Badgastein," he instructed her, "and enquire if I (and you also) can stay there". He asked her to mention this message only to her parents, not to reply, and wait for his next airmail letter or telegram. On 16 November he sent a cable: "Starting aeroplane arriving Badgastein twenty second arrange lodging and meet me ...". He spent a month and a half—from 22 November 1937 to 8 January 1938—with Emilie at his favourite resort of Badgastein.[33]

He goes on to write:
> On 26 December 1937, Subhas Chandra Bose secretly married Emilie Schenkl. Despite the obvious anguish, they chose to keep their relationship and marriage a closely guarded secret.[34]

Leonard A. Gordon, who has written a biography of Netaji and his brother Sarat Chandra Bose, writes:

> Although we must take Emilie Schenkl at her word (about her secret marriage to Bose in 1937), there are a few nagging doubts about an actual marriage ceremony because there is no document that I have seen and no testimony by any other person. ... Other biographers have written that Bose and Miss Schenkl were married in 1942, while Krishna Bose, implying 1941, leaves the date ambiguous. The strangest and most confusing testimony comes from A. C. N. Nambiar, who was with the couple in Badgastein briefly in 1937, and was with them in Berlin during the war as second-in-command to Bose. In an answer to my question about the marriage, he wrote to me in 1978: "I cannot state anything definite about the marriage of Bose referred to by you, since I came to know of it only a good while after the end of the last world war ... I can imagine the marriage having been a very informal one ... So what are we left with? ... We know they had a close passionate relationship and that they had a child, Anita, born 29 November 1942, in Vienna. ... And we have Emilie Schenkl's testimony that they were married secretly in 1937. Whatever the precise dates, the most important thing is the relationship."[35]

According to Fay, Emilie had begun living with Bose almost from the moment he reached Europe. Since Bose had taken a vow that he would not marry until India was free, he was naturally reluctant to formalise their relationship. However, Emilie wanted to get married, and he could not refuse her. But he agonised over the repercussions when the secret became known, as it was bound to some day. Many years later, soon after the debacle at Imphal, during a rare moment when he was alone with Laksmi Swaminathan, he asked her, *"Do you think people in India will understand?"*[36]

Q9. Was Azad Hind Government a Sovereign State?
On 21 October 1943, Bose announced the formation of the *Arzi Hukumat-*

e-Azad Hind, or the Provisional Government of Free India, with himself as the Head of State, Prime Minister and Minister of War. (This was the second Provisional Government of Free India, the first having been established in Kabul on 1 December 1915 by Raja Mahendra Pratap Singh, with the support of Germany, Turkey and Afghanistan. The Provisional Government ceased to function in 1920 when King Amanullah of Afghanistan made peace with England after his famous war of independence.) The INA was declared to be the army of *Azad Hind*. Immediately after its formation, the Provisional Government of Free India declared war against the Allied forces on the Indo-Burma Front. The Azad Hind Government also produced its own currency, postage stamps, court and civil code, and was recognised by some Axis powers. To qualify as a sovereign state, the Azad Hind Government needed some territory of its own. In 1942, the Japanese took possession of Andaman and Nicobar Islands. A year later, the Provisional Government of Azad Hind and the INA were established in the Islands with Lt Col. A.D. Loganathan as Governor General. The islands were renamed *Shaheed* (Martyr) and *Swaraj* (Independence). However, the Provisional Government's civil authority was never enacted in areas occupied by the INA; instead, Japanese military authority prevailed and responsibility for administration of occupied areas of India was shared between the Japanese and the Indian forces. During his interrogation after the war, Loganathan admitted that he had only had control over the islands' education department, as the Japanese had retained full control over the police force, and in protest, he had refused to accept responsibility for any other areas of Government. He could not prevent the Homfreyganj massacre of 30 January 1944, where 44 Indian civilians were shot by the Japanese on suspicion of spying. Many of them were members of the Indian Independence League, whose leader in Port Blair, Dr. Diwan Singh, had already been tortured to death in the Cellular Jail after doing his best to protect the islanders from Japanese atrocities during the first two years of the occupation.[37,38]

Significantly, when the Japanese surrendered at the end of World War II, there was a formal surrender ceremony in which Lt Col. Nathu Singh, who was commanding 1/7 Rajput battalion of the Indian Army, accepted the formal surrender of Japanese troops in the Andaman and Nicobar islands from Vice Admiral Teejo Hara, on behalf of the Supreme Allied Commander, South East Asia.[39]

Can the Azad Hind Government still claim that it was a sovereign state?

Q10. Was Netaji a Military or a Political Leader?

Subhas Chandra Bose was only 24 years old when he returned to India from England in 1921, after having resigned from the ICS. He met Mahatma Gandhi who in turn advised him to meet C.R. Das, who was leading the freedom movement in Bengal. Bose found Das to be more flexible than Gandhi and sympathetic to the extremism that attracted idealistic young men such as Bose in Bengal. It was Das who launched Bose into nationalist politics. For the next 20 years, Bose worked within the ambit of the Indian National Congress politics even as he tried to change its course.[40]

Bose's writings prior to 1939 shows that he disapproved of the racist practices and annulment of democratic institutions in Nazi Germany. However, he expressed admiration for the authoritarian methods which he saw in Italy and Germany during the 1930s, and thought they could be used in building an independent India. During the two years he spent in Germany from 1941 to 1943, he was able to open the Free India Centre in Berlin, and to set up a Free India Radio on which he broadcast every night. He also created the 3,000 strong Free India Legion from Indian prisoners of war captured by Germany's Afrika Korps. This restored his reputation as a politician, which had been adversely affected in the previous two years.

After his arrival in Singapore in 1943, Bose realised that the Japanese were more responsive to his aspirations than the Germans. He was able to obtain more support from Japan than he had from Germany. The Indian National Army that had been disbanded was revived and took part in some operations in Burma alongside Japanese forces. He also created the

Provisional Government of Free India in Japanese occupied Andaman and Nicobar Islands. These efforts did not bear fruit and after the recapture of Singapore by British forces and the surrender of the remnants of the INA at Rangoon, Bose escaped to Manchuria, hoping to continue his campaign for liberating India with the help of the Soviet Union. His life ended in the plane before he could complete his journey.

There is little doubt that Bose had all the qualities needed by a successful political leader. He was confident of his abilities and just a week after his arrival in Singapore said so himself. On 9 July, 60,000 people stood in pouring rain to hear Bose proclaim: *"There is no nationalist leader in India who can claim to possess the many sided experience that I have been able to acquire."*[41]

But can the same be said about his military experience? He had not undergone any military training at all, yet when he raised the INA he chose to be its Commander-in-Chief. He emulated Adolf Hitler, not only in his actions but also in matters of dress, salutation and title. Hitler had some military experience having served in the German Army during World War I, and had risen to rank of corporal. He often overruled his marshals with disastrous results, which ultimately led to his downfall.

During the Imphal campaign, though the Japanese appreciated the firmness with which Bose's forces continued to fight, they were endlessly exasperated with him. A number of Japanese officers, even those like Fujiwara, who were devoted to the Indian cause, saw Bose as a military incompetent as well as an unrealistic and stubborn man who saw only his own needs and problems and could not see the larger picture of the war as the Japanese had to.[42]

Fujiwara, who knew the INA and its leaders more than any other Japanese officer, writes: *"As leader of the Army, Bose became the foundation of spiritual strength and was the pivot of the INA organisation. However, the standard of his operational tactics was, it must be said with great regret, low. He was inclined to be idealistic and not realistic."*

To this Toye adds: *"The fact that he was neither a good soldier, nor the infallible political genius his disciples believed, makes only the more remarkable his power of fascination."*[43]

Though Bose had worn the mantle of a military leader, in Germany as well as in Singapore, some of his actions show that he was not aware of the responsibilities that such a role entails. One of these was the safety and well-being of the men under his command, which is part of the motto of every Indian officer who passes out from the portals of the Indian Military Academy.

After having created the Indian Foreign Legion in Germany, when he found that the Germans were not willing to give him the role that he wanted, he left for Singapore, to seek the help of Japan. He left 3,000 soldiers of the Indian Foreign Legion to their fate. He did something similar when he found that the INA had failed to achieve its objectives. Ten days before the INA surrendered to British forces at Rangoon, Bose left for Manchuria, along with the women of the Rani Jhansi Regiment and a few others. He left 10,000 soldiers of the INA to their fate. This was contrary to the time-honoured custom of a commander always surrendering with his troops, instead of leaving them to their fate.

America declared its independence in 1776, but it took another five years to win freedom from the British. On 19 October 1781, the British General Charles Cornwallis surrendered in Yorktown, Virginia along with 8,000 British troops. During World War I, in the siege of Kut-al Amara, Major General Charles Townshend surrendered to the Turkish forces on 29 April 1916. He spent the rest of the war confined at Constantinople, while around 4,000 of the 10,000 troops which surrendered at Kut died either on the march to Turkish prison camps, or were worked to death in the camps. During World War II, Lieutenant General Arthur Percival surrendered at Singapore to the Japanese along with 136,000 men in February 1942. Churchill called it "the worst disaster in British history". A more recent example is the surrender of Lieutenant General Niazi along with 93,000 Pakistani soldiers at Dacca in 1971, after the liberation of East Pakistan by the Indian Army. Bose may not be aware of this military custom, but surely his military advisers must have been. It is surprising than none of them advised him about this tradition.

Shahnawaz mentions an interesting incident that occurred on 29 April 1945 during the journey after Bose left Rangoon. He writes: *"General Isoda of the Liasion Department asked Netaji to go in the car and the Rani Jhansi girls in the lorries. He said "Do you think I am Ba Maw of Burma that I will leave my men and run for safety?"*[44]

In fact, this is exactly what Bose was doing—leaving his men and running for safety.

Q11. Did the INA Play a Part in India's Independence?

Most INA veterans assert that they played a stellar role in India's independence from British rule. In support of this view, they cite various documents that show that one of the reasons that prompted the British decision to grant independence to India was the realisation that they could no longer rely on the Indian Army. In a note written in early 1946 Lord Wavell wrote: *"It would not be wise to try the Indian Army too highly in suppression of its own people."*[45] In the Foreword to K.C. Praval's book on the Indian Army, Lieutenant General S.K. Sinha wrote, *'There had also been the Naval mutiny at Bombay and the Army (Signals) mutiny at Jubbulpore. It was now clear as daylight to the British that they could no longer use the Indian Army to perpetuate their imperial rule over India ..."*[46]

Menezes writes: *"Now in early 1946, serious cases of mutiny suddenly occurred in the Royal Indian Navy (RIN), less serious in the Royal Air Force (RAF) (wanting early repatriation) and in the Royal Indian Air Force, and a lesser protest in the Indian Army, at Jubbulpore in the Signal Training Centre."*[47] Though Menezes calls the Jubbulpore mutiny 'a lesser protest', in fact it was taken most seriously by the British authorities. The RIN and RIAF at that time were minuscule forces, with hardly any role in governance. The major instrument of British power was the Indian Army, and disaffection in its ranks was a cause for concern, however small. On 28 March 1946, less than a month after the suppression of the mutiny at Jubbulpore, Field Marshal Sir Claude Auchinleck, the Commander-in-Chief in India, broadcast his famous appeal to all officers of the Indian Army. On 30 March 1946, the *Hindustan Times* commented editorially on the Auk's appeal. *"There is no doubt whatever that if the transfer of power is not quickly brought about, the foreign rulers of India cannot count upon the loyalty of the Indian Army...."*[48]

While there is no doubt that nationalist feelings had taken root in the Indian Army, there is no proof that the INA was the catalyst. There were three prominent mutinies in 1946—the RIN mutiny at Bombay, Karachi and other places; the Army mutiny at Jabalpur and the RIAF mutiny at several places. The root causes of all three were deficiencies in pay, food, accommodation, etc; delay in demobilisation and discrimination against Indian servicemen. While it is true that after the INA trials—not before—there was a feeling of sympathy for the INA prisoners in certain quarters in the Armed Forces, there is nothing on record to show any direct correlation between these movements and the INA. In fact, after the fall of Rangoon, so strong was the feeling against the INA prisoners amongst Indian soldiers that Auchinleck had to issue instructions for their safety. The assertion that these mutinies were inspired by the INA appears to be fallacious.

Notes

1. Stephen Cohen, *The Indian Army: Its Contribution to the Development of a Nation*, p. 152.
2. Major General Shahid Hamid, *Disastrous Twilight*, London, 1986, p. 17.
3. Maj Gen Shah Nawaz Khan, *My Memories of INA & its Netaji*, Delhi, Rajkamal Publications, 1946, p. 47.
4. Lt Gen Harbaksh Singh, *In the Line of Duty – A Soldier Remembers*, New Delhi, Lancer, 2000, p. 134.
5. Harbaksh Singh, pp. 111-12.
6. Cohen, p. 149.
7. Gerard H. Corr, *The War of the Springing Tigers*, London, Osprey Publishing House, 1975, p. 149.
8. Shah Nawaz, p. 89.
9. Corr, p. 165.
10. Corr, p. 166.
11. Shah Nawaz, p. 159.
12. RM Kasliwal, *The Impact of Netaji and INA on India's Independence*, p. 20.
13. Stephen Cohen, *The Indian Army: Its Contribution to the Development of a Nation*, p. 152.
14. John Connell, *Auchinleck—A Critical Biography*, p. 97.
15. Hugh Toye, *The Springing Tiger*, London, Cassell Publishers, 1959, p. 120.
16. Captain SS Yadav, *Forgotten Warriors of Indian War of Independence 1941-1946*, (Indian National Army), Gurgaon, 2005, p. 50.
17. Toye, pp. 125-26.
18. Lt. Gen. S.L. Menezes, *Fidelity and Honour—The Indian Army from the Seventeenth to the Twenty-First Century*, New Delhi, Penguin, 1993, p. 397.
19. Hugh Toye, *The Springing Tiger*, p. viii.

20. Maj. Gen. Mohan Singh, *Soldiers' Contribution to Indian Independence*, Army Educational Stores, New Delhi, 1974, p. 65.
21. Bisheshwar Prasad (ed.), *Official History of the Indian Armed Forces in the Second World War 1939-45—India and the War*, History Division, Ministry of Defence, New Delhi, 1966, p. 35.
22. John Connell, *Auchinleck – A Critical Biography*, Cassel & Company, 1959, p. 817.
23. Maj Gen Shahid Hamid, *Disastrous Twilight*, London, 1986, p. 17.
24. Peter Ward Fay, *The Forgotten Army*, University of Michigan Press, 1993, p. 424.
25. Toye, p. 112. (Durrani survived and was later decorated with the George Cross for his fortitude.)
26. Toye, p. 94.
27. Toye, p. 95.
28. Toye, p. 98.
29. Toye, p. 133.
30. Toye, p. 162.
31. Fay, p. 195.
32. Toye, p. 75.
33. Sugata Bose, *His Majesty's Opponent: Subhas Chandra Bose and India's Struggle against Empire*, (Harvard University Press, 2011), p. 127.
34. Bose, 2011, pp. 129-30.
35. Leonard A. Gordon, *Brothers against the Raj: a biography of Indian nationalists Sarat and Subhas Chandra Bose* (Columbia University Press, 1990), pp. 344-45.
36. Fay, p. 312.
37. Jayant Dasgupta, *Japanese in Andaman & Nicobar Islands. Red Sun over Black Water* (Delhi: Manas Publications, 2002), pp. 67, 87, 91-95.
38. L. P. Mathur, *Kala Pani. History of the Andaman & Nicobar Islands with a study of India's Freedom Struggle* (Delhi: Eastern Book Corporation, 1985), pp. 249-51.
39. Major General V.K. Singh, *Leadership in the Indian Army—Biographies of Twelve Soldiers* (New Delhi, Sage Publications, 2005), p. 65.
40. Gordon, 1990, p. 69.
41. Toye, p. 82.
42. Gordon, 1990, p. 517.
43. Toye, p. 178.
44. Shahnawaz, p. 243.
45. Wavell, *The Viceroy's Journal*, London, Oxford University Press, 1973, p. 197.
46. Major KC Praval, *Indian Army after Independence*, New Delhi, Lancer Publishers, 2009, p. ix.
47. Menezes, p. 404.
48. Hamid, p. 47.

8
Nationalism in The Indian Army

The British arrived in India as traders in the middle of the seventeenth century and it was only a hundred years later that they began to recruit Indians as soldiers, leading to the birth of the Indian Army. In fact, the French had begun recruiting Indians to supplement their forces in southern India even earlier. Due to prolonged hostilities between Britain and France, neither nation could spare adequate troops from the homeland and had perforce to depend on local levies to protect their possessions in India from predatory attacks from each other. With time, Indian soldiers began to be used in conflicts with Indian rulers, and the consequent expansion of the territory under the control of the East India Company. In 1757 Robert Clive defeated Siraj-ud-Daula at Plassey with the help of Indian soldiers who had been trained and equipped in the European fashion. Shortly afterwards, the Mughal Emperor conferred on the East India Company the *diwani* (authority to collect revenue) of Bengal, Bihar and Orissa. With this, the Company's main occupation changed from trading to governance. This also conferred on the Company's rule over the provinces a measure of legality.[1]

For almost 200 years after Plassey, Indian soldiers helped the British in establishing their dominion over India and fighting their wars across the borders and high seas. The majority of the men who volunteered to serve under British officers did so for pay, perquisites and status. Most of these men came from families with a tradition of soldiering, whose forefathers had served in the armies of their native chieftains even before the arrival of the British. Almost the whole of the Bengal Army before 1857 comprised Brahmins and Rajputs from Oudh, known colloquially as *Purbias* (men from the East). Many *Purbias* also served in the Scindia's army that fought

British forces under Arthur Wellesley in 1803 at Assaye and at Laswari, after the battle of Delhi. In these engagements, the *Purbias* fought with distinction from both sides, just as they would have under the flags of local chieftains. At that time and even later, Indian soldiers readily joined any army where the pay was good and their religion and caste were respected. Soldiers from foreign lands also found military service in India attractive, and often proved more trustworthy than natives. The Afghan bodyguard of Rani Laxmi Bai of Jhansi remained with her till the end in 1858, displaying commendable courage and gallantry.

Though large parts of the subcontinent had been unified under the Mughals, the concept of nationalism as understood today did not exist. The army of Aurangzeb, the last of the Great Mughals, comprised 300,000 cavalry and 600,000 foot soldiers. However, very few of these were imperial troops. Each of the 15 or 16 *rajas* (chieftains) who fought under his flag brought along 25,000 horsemen or foot soldiers or a combination of the two. These soldiers owed allegiance not to the Mughal Emperor but to their own *raja*, who paid their salaries. Soldiers from princely states such as Jodhpur or Jaipur, though fighting under the Mughal flag, had no feeling of nationalism or patriotism, such as what they displayed when their own lands or kingdoms were threatened. The stories of the gallantry displayed by Rajput soldiers during the three attacks on Chittor are the stuff of legend. Knowing that they would not survive, the men rode out to die at the hands of the enemy after their women had committed *jauhar* (collective self-immolation). The readiness of these soldiers to die for their land and their king was a manifestation of their loyalty and devotion, akin to what is known today as nationalism.

After the decline of the Mughal Empire, the next unification occurred almost a hundred years later, when British control extended to almost the whole of India. With the gradual reduction or disappearance of the armies of native princes, it was only under the British that Indians had the opportunity for military service. The soldier in the Company's Army was not fired by patriotism of the kind felt when he fought for his liege lord. Nevertheless, he served loyally because he had to be true to his salt.

In return for providing him with a means of livelihood, the Company was entitled to his allegiance. By and large, the Indian soldier did not betray the trust of his British masters. But when his religion or caste was under threat, he had no compunction in turning against his officers. On their part, the British took pains to permit the native soldier the greatest latitude in observing his customs and prejudices. On the rare occasions when they failed to do so, the result was catastrophic, as happened in 1857.

The status of the Indian soldier during the British Raj has been the subject of debate among historians and political leaders. There are many who feel that Indians who served in the army under British rule were mercenaries. This was the reason cited by many soldiers for joining the Indian National Army after their capture by the Japanese during World War II. As already mentioned, during the period of British rule the Indian soldier readily joined any army where the pay was good and his religion and caste not under threat. This applied to soldiers serving under the British as well as Indian princes. The example of *Purbias* in the Scindia's army has already been cited. It is interesting to recall that the primary reason that impelled most British soldiers to serve in India was the attraction of prize money, which was shared among all ranks after a victory. The British system of prize money was a euphemism for institutionalised robbery and plunder of the wealth of the vanquished by the victor. After the recapture of Delhi by British forces in 1858, the booty collected by the prize agents was worth a million and a quarter sterling. If anything, the British soldier serving in India was more of a mercenary that his native colleague.

After the grant of the *diwani* of Bengal, Bihar and Orissa in 1765, the status of the East India Company became that of a vassal of the Mughal Emperor. The right to collect revenue automatically conferred the responsibility for administration, including maintenance of law and order, for which the requirement of an army was indisputable. Legally, the British were no longer foreign intruders but local chieftains, acting on behalf of the Mughal Court. Viewed from this angle, the Company's Army was similar to those maintained by other native rulers. Naturally, soldiers who opted to serve in such an army could not be termed as mercenaries. In fact, in

1922 a British historian, F. W. Buckler, presented a paper on the Mutiny of 1857 at the Royal Historical Society, in which he expressed the legal view that it was the Company, as the '*dewan*' of the Mughal Emperor, that had mutinied against the Emperor Bahadur Shah.[2]

After 1857, the responsibility for governing India was taken over by the British Government. With this, the status of the British in India also changed. India was now a colony, a part of the mighty British Empire and the "brightest jewel in the Crown" of the British monarch. Even during this period, it is doubtful if Indian soldiers serving under the British can be called mercenaries. By definition, a mercenary soldier fights for money or reward for a country other than his own. Though Indian soldiers served under British officers, it is a debatable point if they were fighting for a country other than their own. While the Indian mutiny in 1857 was to a considerable extent inspired by the desire to be free of British rule, the concept of nationalism among the general public took root only after the birth of the Congress at the turn of the century and flowered only after the Civil Disobedience Movement in 1930 and the Quit India Movement in 1942.

Britain depended on the Indian Army to maintain her control over India. As a result, Indian troops were frequently employed to control disturbances inspired by the freedom struggle. This sometimes brought them into conflict with their compatriots, who questioned their lack of patriotism and branded them as mercenaries. However, it is pertinent to record that from the time the British government assumed the responsibility for governing India, the primary role of the Indian Army was the defence of India against invasion from the north-west, with Russia or Afghanistan being the most likely adversaries. After World War I the size of the Indian Army had to be drastically reduced due to financial constraints and a reduction in the external threat. In 1921 the Central Legislative Assembly discussed the role of the Indian Army and determined that it should not be used for imperial campaigns outside India. But it was naïve to expect that if the need arose, Britain would hesitate to call upon the resources of the largest and richest colony of the Empire. In 1933 the War Office spelt out the role of the Indian Army in the following words:

The duties of the army in India include the preservation of internal security in India, the covering of the lines of internal communication, and the protection of India against external attack. Though the scale of forces is not calculated to meet external attack by a great Power, their duties might well comprise the initial resistance to such an attack pending the arrival of imperial reinforcements.[3]

The role of the Indian Army was thus enhanced from being purely for the defence of India to include a supplementary role of acting as an Imperial Reserve. The British Government agreed to grant an annual subsidy of 1.5 million pounds to the Government of India for this purpose. By 1938 the threat of war had become clear and the Government of India requested London to reconsider both the military and financial aspects of her defence problems, and conclude a fresh contract between Britain and India in which the latter's financial limitations were recognised. The Imperial Defence Committee constituted a subcommittee under Major General Henry Pownall to report on the defence problems of India. The Pownall committee reported that the changed strategic situation and development of modern armaments, particularly air forces, warranted a more important role for India in defence of vital areas on the Imperial lines of communication in the Middle and Far East. It recommended the unconditional allocation of one Indian division as a strategic reserve for use of the Imperial Government wherever required. Based on this, the Imperial defence Council issued the 1938 Plan (Document No. B-43746) which envisaged six tasks for the defence forces of India, namely, defence of the Western Frontier against external aggression; defence of land frontiers other than the Western Frontier; maintenance of law and order and the suppression of disorder and rebellion; safeguarding strategic lines of communication within India; provision of a general reserve with mobile components; and provision of forces for possible employment overseas at the request of the Government in UK.

It is pertinent to note that the primary responsibility of the Indian Army—defence of India—never changed. The employment of Indian troops overseas was covered by a formal contract between the governments of UK and India. Troops are often sent overseas in accordance with treaties, contracts or agreements between two countries. Sometimes, such help is extended even without the existence of formal treaties. Troops from Canada, Australia, New Zealand, South Africa and India fought for Britain in World War II in accordance with agreements and contracts between these nations. To counter the threat of the Axis powers, nations such as UK, France, Russia, China and USA made temporary alliances and fought as allies. Even after Independence, India has continued to assist other nations who have asked for military assistance in controlling internal problems. Examples are the dispatch of Indian troops to Maldives and Sri Lanka in the 1980s. In recent years, troops from several nations have participated in the operations in Vietnam, Afghanistan, Kuwait and Iraq. These troops cannot be termed mercenaries, since they fought in foreign lands not of their own volition but at the behest of their respective countries. The Indian soldiers who were sent abroad during the British Raj did not volunteer for Foreign Service in an individual capacity; they were sent for assignments abroad by their employers, namely, the Government of India.

Apart from the Indian soldiers in the regular army, troops from the forces maintained by Indian princely states also formed part of the contingents sent for Imperial service during both World Wars. According to the Imperial Service Troops Scheme of 1888, specific units were earmarked for Imperial purposes and organised to Indian Army establishments. In 1914 the strength of the Imperial Service troops was 22,613. Ultimately, 20 mounted regiments and 13 battalions were offered for service during World War I. During World War II, the assistance provided by Indian princely states was significantly higher. In 1945, there were 41,463 soldiers from Indian State Forces in Indian Government service out of a total of 99,367, which was more than 40 per cent of their strength.[4]

The assistance provided by India to Britain during World War II was not gratis. The Modernisation Committee under Major General Claude

Auchinleck set up in 1938 was followed by the Expert Committee on Defence of India under Admiral of the Fleet, Lord Alfred Chatfield in 1939. When World War II started, various measures recommended by these committees had just been taken in hand. To meet the cost of modernisation and increase India's output of explosives and ammunition, the British Government made a grant of 25 million pounds and a loan of 9 million pounds. Shortly after the outbreak of the war, an agreement was signed between London and New Delhi on the sharing of cost of Indian forces utilised for imperial defence. According to the Defence Expenditure Agreement of November 1939 India was committed to contributing to the total expenditure a sum equivalent to her normal peacetime expenditure on defence plus the cost of operations undertaken in defence of purely Indian interests and a share of the measures undertaken jointly in the interests of Indian and Imperial Defence. Everything over and above this would be met by Britain. By the time the war ended, Britain's debt to India was more than 1,000 million pounds.[5]

Indian soldiers played an important role in Britain's victory over her adversaries in World War I and II, during which they fought valiantly in theatres around the globe, suffering substantial casualties and earning many gallantry awards. At the same time, the struggle for independence from British rule continued unabated, spearheaded by the Indian National Congress. It is interesting to note the attitude of the political leaders to military service under the British. During World War I, when the Viceroy appealed to Indians to come forward and enlist, his call was supported by the political leaders of the day, including Gandhi and Tilak. Following the Civil Disobedience Movement in 1930 and the Quit India Movement in 1942, many Indian officers with nationalistic feelings had misgivings about military service under British rule. Nonetheless, they continued to serve for many reasons. The primary role of the Indian Army was to defend India, and service in the Army could not be termed as anti-national. Secondly, the political leaders who were then heading the freedom struggle had decided to support Britain during the War, after being assured that India would be given dominion status once it was over. Many soldiers were affected by the freedom struggle, and contemplated leaving the service to join it. However, they were invariably dissuaded by the far-sighted political leaders of the day.

In a speech at Poona in 1916, Bal Gangadhar Tilak said: *"If you want Home Rule be prepared to defend your home. Had it not been for my age I would have been the first to volunteer. You cannot reasonably say that the ruling will be done by you and the fighting for you—by Europeans or Japanese, in the matter of Home Defence. Show ... that you are willing to take advantage of the opportunity offered to you by the Viceroy to enlist in an Indian Citizen's Army. When you do that, your claim for having the commissioned ranks opened to you will acquire double weight."*[6]

Second Lieutenant (later Major General) A.A. Rudra passed out from the Temporary School for Indian Cadets, also known as the Daly Cadet College, Indore on 1 December 1919, along with 38 others officers, including K.M. Cariappa, who was to become the first Indian Commander-in-Chief. Before joining the Daly Cadet College in 1918, Rudra had fought at Ypres and Somme in World War I as a member of the Universities and Public Schools Brigade. En route to join his battalion—the 28th Punjabis, then stationed near Jerusalem in Palestine—Rudra spent a month's leave with his father, Prof. S.K. Rudra, who was then Principal of St. Stephen's College, Delhi. At that time Mahatma Gandhi was staying as a house guest. In fact, after returning from South Africa, Gandhi stayed in Prof. Rudra's house for nine years, from 1915 to 1923, before moving to the Bhangi Colony. During his leave, while bicycling through Chandni Chowk, the young Rudra was horrified when he saw British troops using force to suppress the violent protests after the Jallianwala Bagh incident. He decided to resign his commission and sought Gandhi's advice.

That evening Rudra sought out the Mahatma, who shared his father's study. Unburdening his doubts and dismays, Rudra asked Gandhi for his advice—whether he should or should not hold a commission in the British-Indian Army. Without giving a direct answer, Gandhi told Rudra that he was a grown up, mature man, not a child; he had fought for three years in the Great War and faced dangers and difficulties. It was for him to make up his own mind and act accordingly. Rudra replied that he had been away from India for six years and was unaware of the political changes that had taken place during his absence. He wanted to know what would happen if there was a fight for independence, and he found himself on the wrong side. Gandhi said: *"How can we ever hope to rid ourselves of the British by force of arms? We are a poor, uneducated, unarmed people—we can never fight the British. But do not despair. I know my Englishman. He will deal with us honourably. When the time is ripe and if our cause is a righteous one and if our country is ready for it, he will give us our freedom on a platter. And then, when we are a free country, we shall have to have an army."* Indirect as it was, Rudra took it as a green light to remain in the Army.[7]

In September 1926, after passing out from Sandhurst, Second Lieutenant (later Lieutenant General) S.P.P. Thorat and a few of his colleagues were returning from UK on the P&O liner *Kaiser-i-Hind*. On the same ship were two well-known Indians—Lala Lajpat Rai and Mohammed Ali Jinnah. As Thorat recalls in his memoirs, both of them took a paternal interest in the newly commissioned Indian officers. Lajpat Rai asked Thorat to correct the proofs of his latest book, *Unhappy India*. One day Thorat asked him, *"Sir, do you think that we have done wrong in joining the Indian Army on the strength of which the British are ruling us?"* Lalaji thought for a while and then replied, *"No, I don't think so at all. How long will the British continue to rule us? One day, India shall become a free country, and then we will need trained men like you. So work hard and qualify yourself for that moment."*[8]

In 1928, Captain (later General) K.S. Thimayya's battalion, 4/19 Hyderabad, moved from Baghdad to Allahabad. Thimayya spent a few days in Bombay, en route, where he met Sarojini Naidu, who introduced him to Jinnah. This was Thimayya's first contact with nationalist leaders, and he found the experience confusing. As an Indian, he sympathised with their cause. But as a soldier, he had sworn an oath of allegiance to the British sovereign. He was not sure if he could reconcile his position, with respect to his country, and his profession. At Allahabad, he came into close contact with the Nehrus, and was a frequent guest at Anand Bhawan, where he came to know Nehru's sisters, Vijaya Lakshmi Pandit and Krishna (Betty) Hutheesingh. He also met Dr. Kailash Nath Katju and Sir Tej Bahadur

Sapru. After the Civil Disobedience Movement in 1930, there was a general upsurge of nationalist feeling among the people. Thimayya was deeply impressed by the winds of nationalism then blowing through the country, and the sacrifices being made by the people. On one occasion, he almost got into trouble, for throwing his peak cap in a bonfire of British goods, at the behest of Krishna Hutheesingh. One day, he and some other Indian officers met Moti Lal Nehru and told him that they wanted to resign their commissions. The elder Nehru told them not to do so. *"There are enough of us in the Congress, and we need more people in the Army"*, he said, advising them to stick it out. He felt that the Indianisation of the Army had been achieved after much effort and should not be stopped. He added: *"We're going to win independence. Perhaps not this year or the next, but sooner or later the British will be driven out. When that happens, India will stand alone. We will have no one to protect us but ourselves. It is then that our survival will depend on men like you."*[9]

During the Quit India Movement in 1942, Mahatma Gandhi was interned at the Aga Khan Palace at Poona, under the direct care of Colonel M.G. Bhandari, of the Army Medical Corps, the father-in-law of Captain (later Lieutenant General) P.S. Bhagat, who had recently won the Victoria Cross. Accompanied by his colleague, Arjan Singh, Prem Bhagat went to meet the great man, and asked him how they could help in the freedom movement. Gandhiji gave them almost the same answer that he had given Second Lieutenant Rudra more than 20 years earlier. He advised Bhagat and his friends to continue in their chosen profession. He said that once the country became free, it would require the services of dedicated professional soldiers.[10]

Along with Mahatma Gandhi, almost all prominent Congress leaders were imprisoned during the Quit India Movement in 1942. This caused resentment in the great majority of Indian soldiers and officers, many of them being imbued with nationalistic feelings for the first time. One such officer was Second Lieutenant Dadachanji, who was posted in the training battalion of the 15th Punjabis, located in Ambala. He was a Parsee, who had been studying in England when war broke out, and volunteered for enlistment. After the political disturbances in the wake of the Cripps Mission, the battalion was put on alert and ordered to have one company on permanent standby for internal security duties. When Dadachanji was detailed to command a flying column, he refused. He was promptly put under arrest by his company commander for treason, and subsequently marched up before the commanding officer, Major A.A. Rudra. When asked the reasons for his refusal to do duty, Dadachanji stated firmly and indignantly that he had joined the Army voluntarily to fight Germans, not to shoot down his own countrymen; he was not going to take part in any internal security duty that might involve shooting Indians. Rudra was impressed by his moral courage; he ruled out the charge of treason and released Dadachanji from arrest. The case was forwarded to the brigade commander, who also took a liberal view of the case. By the time the matter reached District Headquarters at Lahore, large-scale violence had erupted in the wake of the Quit India Movement. The authorities decided to hush up the matter and advised him to resign. Dadachanji agreed, albeit reluctantly.[11]

Among the political leaders of that period, the only one who advocated violence as a means of achieving freedom was Subhas Chandra Bose. However, according to Commodore B.K. Dang, his views were similar to those of others as far as military service under the British was concerned. Dang had done his training as a marine engineer on the training ship *Dufferin* before the outbreak of World War II. When the war started he volunteered and was accepted in the Royal Indian Navy. He was sent to Calcutta for an engineering course and was staying with a friend who was a socialist. When they came to know that Subhas Bose was living nearby under house arrest, Dang and his colleagues expressed a desire to meet him. Bose came to the house just behind the one where they were staying to meet Dang and his friends. One of them was C.G.K. Reddy, who later joined the *Deccan Herald*, becoming a close associate of George Fernandes and subsequently a member of the Rajya Sabha. When Dang and his friends told Bose that they wanted to join the freedom movement, he advised them to stick on in the Navy and get trained so that when the British left they could take over from the British.

Although the struggle for freedom had been going on for almost half a century, the Indian armed forces remained virtually untouched until the outbreak of World War II, when a large number of Indians were granted emergency commissions. Though Indians had been given commissions earlier, their number was small. Moreover, most of them came from feudal or military families, which were largely unaffected by political events. On the other hand, the majority of Emergency Commissioned Officers came from rural or urban middle class backgrounds, which were the most active constituents of the freedom movement. Due to their upbringing, lack of training and political leanings, the Emergency Commissioned Officers were not treated as equals by British officers. This discriminatory attitude was largely responsible for the growth of disaffection and nationalistic fervour among Indian officers during World War II. Another reason that caused frustration among Indian officers was the perceived delay in the process of Indianisation, which seemed to progressing at a very slow pace, mainly due to opposition by British officers.

It may appear strange, but many people connected with the freedom movement did not hesitate to send their sons to serve in the Army. One such person was Dr. Christopher Barretto, a leading dental surgeon of Nagpur, who was frequently summoned to Wardha to treat Mahatma Gandhi. His son, Terence Barretto, joined the Army and was commissioned in the Indian Signal Corps in 1940, retiring as a brigadier in 1965. Terence recalls that Mahatma Gandhi often referred patients to his father, requesting him not to charge them for his services, as they were members of his growing family of 'national beggars'. Among the 'national beggars' treated by Dr. Barretto were Mahadev Desai, the Mahatma's secretary, and Khan Abdul Ghaffar Khan, the Frontier Gandhi. Terence Barretto was himself a die-hard nationalist, who was constantly in trouble for his anti-British views, being once put on 'adverse report' by his commanding officer in Burma. He had frequent tiffs with British officers on minor issues such as playing Indian music or eating Indian food in the mess. He recalls that Indian officers keenly followed the activities of leaders of the freedom movement and discussed among themselves the future of the country. He had in his possession the copy of the *Amrita Bazar Patrika* of 26 January 1947, which he purchased in Chittagong, containing a full page (in colour) of the Congress flag, with the Indian Independence Pledge in bold print. On the reverse of the page is 'Sixty Years of Congress' by Dr. Pattabhi Sitaramayya. Barretto and his colleagues hung the flag in their room behind a curtain.

The most well-known nationalist soldier was Lieutenant General Thakur Nathu Singh, a Sandhurst trained King's Commissioned Indian Officer who had been christened 'Fauji Gandhi' by his colleagues. Even as a young officer, Nathu Singh openly expressed his anti- British feelings, for which he was often in trouble. When he was a major, he was asked to suppress an agitation during the Quit India Movement in 1942. Nathu Singh objected, saying that it was not fair to ask him to shoot at his own countrymen, who were only asking for their freedom. He requested the Commanding Officer to give the job to some other officer, but this was refused, and he was told that if he disobeyed orders he would be court-martialled. Nathu Singh refused to carry out the orders, and the matter was reported to the District Commander, Major General Bruce Scott. When he was marched up to General Scott, Nathu Singh defended his action, as a 'conscientious objector', quoting the example of similar cases in Ireland. To his good luck, Scott turned out to be an Irishman. He appreciated the stand taken by Nathu Singh, and let him off.

Nathu Singh was of the view that the slow process of Indianisation and the discriminatory treatment of Indian officers were largely responsible for the birth of the Indian National Army (INA). He had grave doubts whether the British were serious about Indianisation, or it was merely 'window dressing', to impress the public and the outside world. Despite the fact that two and a half million Indians had fought in two wars, they had not been able to produce a single General. Important appointments dealing with operations were denied to them, and just a handful were given command of units. Drawing a parallel with the Soviet Union, which took shape at about the same time as Indianisation began in India, the disparities were obvious. However, his most scathing comments were reserved for the unfair treatment meted out to Indians, which he covered at length in a strongly worded letter to the Commander-in-Chief, General Auchinleck, on 17 December 1945, soon after the commencement of the INA trials in the Red Fort in Delhi. Nathu Singh, who was then a lieutenant colonel, wrote:

> The formation of the INA was not alone the work of its leaders like Bose, or of the Jap Opportunist. The creation and growth of the INA was a direct result of the continuous unjust treatment of Indian officers in the Army. It is the natural heritage of years of dissatisfaction, disappointment and disgust of various elements in the Indian Army. The present members of the INA are to be blamed for their conduct, but equally to blame is the Imperialist Anti-Indian British element in the army who by their talk and action daily estranged the otherwise loyal mind of the Indian, and last but not least to blame are the British reverses in the Far East, which left the Indian soldiers to their fate.[12]

The growth of nationalism in the armed forces was inevitable, given the sentiments of the general public. To their credit, senior British officers recognised it as a natural consequence of the mood sweeping the country, which touched all sections of society. Writing to Army Commanders after the first INA trials, General Auchinleck wrote: *"In this connection, it should be remembered, I think, that every Indian worthy of the name is today a 'Nationalist', though this does not mean that he is necessarily 'anti-British'. All the same, where India and her independence is concerned there are no pro-British Indians. Every Indian commissioned officer is a Nationalist and rightfully so, provided he hopes to attain independence for India by constitutional means."*[13]

The discontent among Indian officers was noticeable not only in the combat arms, but also in the supporting arms and services. In April 1946, Major General C.H.H. Vulliamy, the Signal Officer-in-Chief addressed a letter to all commanding officers. He wrote: *"Very few ICOs have applied for regular commission. I believe that the main reason for this poor response is that a large majority of the ICOs in the Corps are discontented because they feel that they have been given a raw deal during the war and that this feeling has been engendered mainly due to two causes: discrimination shown by certain COs against ICOs and unsympathetic attitude towards ICOs.*" In another letter addressed to the Chief Signal Officers of Commands, General Vulliamy wrote: "*It appears to me that there is a certain amount of hesitation lower down the chain of command in implementing freely and fully the policy of Indianisation. This lack of trust in ICOs must stop. Either an ICO is fit to be an officer or he is not.*"[14]

The military hierarchy was aware of the discontent and alienation of Indian officers. These issues, coupled with the growing aspirations for independence, became a source of concern. They tried to take remedial measures, but it was too late. By the time World War II ended, Indian officers had become true nationalists. This was one of the most important factors in the British decision to grant complete independence to India, and also to advance the date from June 1948 to August 1947.

Notes
1. Lt Gen S.L. Menezes, *Fidelity & Honour* (New Delhi, 1993), p. 10, quoting M. Moir, *A General Guide to the India Office Records* (London, 1988), p. 3.
2. Menezes, p. 187.
3. Bisheshwar Prasad (ed.), *Official History of the Indian Armed Forces in the Second World War 1939-45—India and the War* (New Delhi, 1966), p. 35.
4. F.W. Perry, *The Commonwealth Armies—Manpower and Reorganization in Two World Wars* (Manchester, 1988), pp. 87, 117.
5. Sir Penderel Moon, *The British Conquest and Dominion of India* (London: Duckworth, 1989), pp. 1093-1094.
6. Stephen C. Cohen, *The Indian Army* (Delhi, 1990), p. 92, quoting *Bal Gangadhar Tilak—His Writings and Speeches*, p. 365.
7. Maj Gen D.K. Palit, *Major General A.A Rudra—His Service in Three Armies and Two World Wars* (New Delhi, 1997), pp. 71-72.
8. Lt Gen S.P.P. Thorat, *From Reveille to Retreat* (New Delhi, 1986), p. 8.
9. Humphrey Evans, *Thimayya of India* (Dehradun, 1988), p. 123.
10. Lt Gen Mathew Thomas and Jasjit Mansingh, *Lt. Gen. P.S. Bhagat, VC* (New Delhi, 1994), p. 102.
11. Palit, pp. 252-54.
12. Maj Gen V.K. Singh, *Leadership in the Indian Army—Biographies of Twelve Soldiers* (New Delhi, 2005), p. 64.

13. Maj Gen Ian Cardozo (ed.), *The Indian Army—A Brief History* (New Delhi, 2005), p. 54.
14. Maj Gen V.K. Singh, *History of the Corps of Signals, Volume II* (New Delhi, 2006), p. 296.

9
Did The Army Signals Mutiny at Jubbulore Play A Part in India's Independence?

---❖---

World War II started on 1 September 1939, when Germany invaded Poland. Two days later, France and the United Kingdom declared war on Germany. India was then a British colony and joined the war, after a proclamation on 3 September 1939 by the Viceroy, Lord Linlithgow. Mahatma Gandhi openly expressed his sympathy for Britain, but the Congress made its support conditional to a promise that India would be granted dominion status, if not complete independence, after the war ended. When no such assurance was given, the Congress decided to resign from the ministries in all provinces. The Muslims were divided on the issue; while the Muslim League warned the British Government that they would support them only if they were given justice and fair play, the Muslim Premiers of Bengal, Punjab and Sind pledged the unconditional support of their provinces. Soon afterwards, Jinnah made the demand for a separate state for the Muslims—Pakistan. This was opposed not only by the Congress but by several prominent Muslims, such as Fazl-ul-Huq and Sir Sikander Hyat Khan. Unfortunately, the Viceroy did not give Jinnah's demand serious thought, choosing to ignore the demand and leave it for someone else to deal with, after the war. In a letter to Lord Zetland, the Secretary of State for India, he wrote, *"I am not too keen to start talking about a period after which British rule will have ceased in India. I suspect that the day is very remote and I feel the least we say about it in all probability the better"*. Later, the well-known historian S. Gopal commented on this passage: *"There could be no more revealing gloss on all the statements made by British authorities over the years on their determination to leave India."*[1]

Linlithgow was not the only British statesman who regarded grant of independence to India as premature; the British Prime Minster, Winston Churchill, was an even greater imperialist. After the fall of France in 1940 and of Singapore and Burma in 1941, British fortunes were at a low ebb. With the Japanese invasion of India becoming a real possibility, it became important for Britain to garner support from the Indian public. In January 1942 Sir Tej Bahadur Sapru, a prominent liberal leader, telegraphed the British Prime Minister, advising him to treat India on par with other units of the Commonwealth. General Chiang Kai-shek, worried that China would be cut off from western aid if India fell, visited India in February to rally Indian opinion against the Japanese, at the end of which he reported to Roosevelt and Churchill that unless the Indian political problem was immediately solved, Japanese attack on India would be "virtually unopposed". A few weeks before the 'Lend Lease' Bill was signed, Roosevelt sent Averell Harriman to London with the message: *"Get out of India, or you may not get what you need now".* Shortly afterwards, Roosevelt wrote to Churchill that American public opinion just could not understand why India could not be granted independence immediately.[2]

Churchill decided to send Sir Stafford Cripps to India with a draft declaration of policy that was designed to convince the Indian people of Britain's sincere resolve to grant them independence as soon as the war was over. During the war, the present set-up would continue, with Britain retaining control for the direction of the war. The declaration was more than what had been offered earlier, and both the Congress and the Muslim league were inclined to accept it. However, Mahatma Gandhi opposed it, since it provided for the provinces and the rulers of princely states, as distinct from the people of these states, the authority to refuse accession, which could result in vivisection of the country. During discussions, it emerged that the proposed Executive Council that was to consist entirely of Indians, except for the Viceroy and the Commander-in-Chief, would have very little say in defence matters. As a result, the declaration was rejected by both the Congress and the Muslim League. Commenting on the episode, Penderel Moon writes:

> The mission had failed, as Linlithgow, Churchill and Amery had expected and may well have hoped. Churchill indeed did not attempt to conceal his pleasure at the outcome. In a consoling telegram to Cripps he said that the effect throughout Britain and the United States had been "wholly beneficial". As a public relations exercise designed to appease American and left-wing British opinion, it was certainly a success. A serious attempt to meet Indian political aspirations had been made, and this was really no less important than that it should succeed—indeed its success should be fraught with positive disadvantages. Congress leaders as members of the Executive Council were likely to be more of an embarrassment than a help in the prosecution of the war, and endless wranglings between them and the League members were more probable than a gradual drawing together in the execution of a common task.[3]

After the failure of the Cripps Mission, the British made no serious attempt to end the deadlock until the war ended. The intervening years saw many political changes, one of the notable ones being the 'Quit India' resolution of 1942, after which almost all Congress leaders were imprisoned and Jinnah gradually emerged as the undisputed leader of the Muslims. There was no apparent change in the British attitude to Indian independence, Linlithgow continuing to hold the view that British rule in India would continue for a long time. *"For many years to come"*, he told L.C.M.S. Amery, the Secretary of State for India, *"our position in India will be the dominating position"*. In the same vein he told William Phillips, an emissary of President Roosevelt, *"there could be no question of our handing over here for very many years"*.[4]

In October 1943 Linlithgow was replaced as Viceroy by Field Marshal Wavell, the post of Commander-in-Chief in India being taken by General Sir Claude Auchinleck, who returned to his old job from the Middle East. Unlike his predecessor, Wavell did not wish to wait for the war to end before finding a solution to the Indian problem. Even before he took up his new appointment, he submitted to London a memorandum recommending the formation of a coalition government in India drawn from all political parties. His proposal was shot down by the epitome imperialist, Prime Minister Winston Churchill. After attending a meeting in which his proposal was discussed, Wavell was convinced that the Cabinet was "not honest in its expressed desire to make progress in India". Not surprisingly, Wavell waited for a year before making any fresh political move in India. During this period, his proposals for appointment of Indians in important positions or upgrading their status were vetoed by London. In September 1944 he sent to the Secretary of State a proposal for a transitional government working within the existing constitution but representative of all political parties. Wavell offered to come to London personally to explain his proposals.

After procrastinating for six months, the Government asked Wavell to come to London, only after a veiled threat to resign if there was any further delay. The next two months were spent in futile discussions with various members of the Cabinet. Churchill's obduracy prevented any worthwhile result until the end of the war in Europe, after which the Coalition was dissolved and a caretaker Conservative Government took office. Churchill suddenly dropped his objections; he subsequently revealed that he had been assured that the move was bound to fail. After he returned to India Wavell invited Gandhi, Jinnah and 20 other political leaders for a conference at Simla, where he placed his proposals before them. Churchill had been right; the conference failed, thanks to Jinnah's intransigence. However, Gandhi, Azad and several others were impressed by Wavell's sincerity. They felt that he had opened new possibilities of Indo-British friendship.[5]

The Second World War came to an end with the capitulation of Japan after the dropping of the atomic bombs on Hiroshima and Nagasaki in August 1945. This coincided with the victory of the Labour party in the general elections in Britain. With Churchill's removal from the scene, the Indian problem began to receive serious attention. Wavell's suggestions to hold elections for the central and provincial assemblies, lift the ban on Congress organisations and release political prisoners were approved and he was asked to come to London for consultations. Sir Penderel Moon gives an interesting hypothesis as to the reasons for the change in Britain's outlook after the war, which explains the central role of the Indian army in bringing about the end of British rule in India. He writes:

> Even before the war British rule over India had become an anachronism, and two of the reasons that had then deterred the British from relaxing their grip had now, as result of the war, lost all validity. One of these was the fear that an independent Indian Government might repudiate all India's foreign debt, most of which was held in England; but by the end of the war this had all been liquidated and Great Britain had become the debtor, owing India over 1,000 million pounds. The second and less selfish reason was that in the pre-war years there were not nearly enough trained Indian military officers to take over the Indian army and provide for India's defence; but now there were over 15,000 trained Indian officers, and though only two or three had reached the rank of brigadier there was a sufficient number of them capable of filling the higher posts except in the technical arms, and plenty of regimental officers.[6]

Towards the end of 1945 Wavell was confronted with a new problem—the trials of three officers of the Indian National Army in the Red Fort at Delhi. During the war people in India and the political parties had virtually ignored the Indian National Army, which had been raised from captured Indian prisoners of war with the help of Japan. After the fall of Rangoon, Subhas Chandra Bose fled to Bangkok—he died in an air crash shortly afterwards—leaving behind the bulk of the officers and men of the Indian National Army who became prisoners. It was decided to segregate them into three groups—white, grey and black—depending on the extent of their involvement. The majority, who fell in the first two categories, were either reinstated or discharged, but those who were accused of serious atrocities were to be tried by court martial. The initial trials were held in Simla and did not attract much notice. About 20 such men were found guilty and executed at Attock before it was decided to shift the trials to Delhi.[7]

The decision to carry out the trials in the Red Fort at Delhi was unwise, as Auchinleck was to lament on several occasions. It gave the Congress a heaven-sent opportunity to arouse popular feeling against the British. The Muslim League also expressed their support for the prisoners, and the Viceroy and Commander-in-Chief were in a dilemma. The three officers were found guilty of waging war against the King, and sentenced to be cashiered and transported for life. The sentences caused great resentment and Auchinleck was forced to commute the sentences of transportation. This had a serious impact, since it divided the Indian Army, where there were many who agreed with the decision while others felt that it amounted to condoning treason, considered the most heinous of military crimes. For the first time in its long history, there were fissures in the Indian Army, which were to have serious consequences in the coming months.

The year 1946 opened with serious cases of disaffection in all three armed services, which have been described in earlier chapters. In the last week of March the Cabinet Mission, comprising Sir Stafford Cripps, the President of the Board of Trade; Mr. A.V. Alexander, First Lord of the Admiralty; and Lord Pethick-Lawrence, the Secretary of State, arrived in Delhi, with the task of reaching an agreement with the principal political parties on two issues: one, the method of framing a constitution for a self-governing, independent India and two, the setting up of a new Executive Council of Interim Government that would hold office while the constitution was being drafted. The Viceroy was fully involved in the deliberations of the Cabinet Mission, but the problem of the disaffection in the armed services caused him not a little anxiety. In a dispatch addressed to King George VI on 22 March 1946, he wrote:

> The last three months have been anxious and depressing. They have been marked by continuous and unbridled abuse of the Government, of the British, of officials and police, in political speeches, in practically the whole of the Press, and in the Assembly; by serious rioting in Bombay; by a mutiny in the RIN, much indiscipline in the RIAF; some unrest in the Army; by an unprecedented drought and famine conditions over many

parts of India; by threatened strikes on the Railways, and in the Posts and Telegraphs; by a general sense of insecurity and lawlessness. ...

The most disturbing feature of all is that unrest is beginning to appear in some units of the Indian Army; so far almost entirely in the technical arms. Auchinleck thinks that the great mass of the Indian Army is still sound, and I believe that this is so. It may not take long, however, to shake their steadiness if the Congress and Muslim League determine to use the whole power of propaganda at their command to do so.[8]

On 27 March 1946, Sir J.A. Thorne, the Home Member of the Viceroy's Council, was asked to prepare a brief appreciation of what would happen if the Cabinet Mission does not achieve a settlement. One of the important points covered was the staunchness of the Indian Services if called upon to quell civil disturbances. According to Thorne's appreciation, which he submitted on 5 April the loyalty of the Services could no longer be taken for granted. In the 1942 disturbances the Services were nearly 100 per cent staunch, but this would not be so on a future occasion. If faced with the prospect of firing on mobs, not all units could be relied upon. As regards the behaviour that could be expected of troops generally under these circumstances, there would be a lot of disaffection, and downright mutiny, especially in the RIAF, RIN and Signals units. Thorne suggested that an appreciation on these aspects be prepared by the War Department.[9]

The Commander-in-Chief directed the Director of Military Intelligence, Brigadier B.P.T. O'Brien, to assess the present state of morale and degree of reliability of the three Indian fighting services, with special reference to the Indian Commissioned Officers, from the point of view of their capacity to act under three conditions—in aid of civil power in widespread communal or anti-present-Government disturbances; in operations on the Frontier; and as garrisons overseas. The Director of Military Intelligence submitted the Note to the Commander-in-Chief on 25 April who expressed his general agreement with its contents. Extracts from the Note are given below:[10]

... We consider that the Indian Services could not remain in being in the face of communal trouble started by, or turned into, a Jehad; neither can we suggest any action which might increase the likelihood of them staying firm under these circumstances.

We consider that the very great bulk of Indian Armoured Corps, Gunners, Sappers and Infantry, could be relied on to act in communal trouble not amounting to a Jehad but would advise against bringing other services in the Army, the R.I.N. or the R.I.A.F. into direct contact with rioters.

... Our views on the reliability of the Indian Services in widespread Congress inspired trouble are
(a) The Indian Armoured Corps, Gunners, Sappers and Infantry can in the main be depended on provided that their I.C.O.s, particularly the senior ones, remain loyal and any waverers among them are dealt with firmly and immediately...
(b) The Indian Signal Corps cannot at present be considered reliable...
(c) The Ancillary Services of the Army as a whole should not be relied on to act against rioters...
(d) The Royal Indian Navy cannot at present be regarded as reliable....
(e) The Royal Indian Air Force must be regarded as doubtful...

... the key to the reliability of the Services, particularly the Army, is the attitude of the I.C.O. ...the morale of the I.C.O. can be greatly improved by the example and attitude of British officers...

Auchinleck forwarded Brigadier O'Brien's Note to the Viceroy and the Cabinet Mission, giving copies to Army Commanders as well as the Chiefs of the Royal Indian Navy and the Royal Indian Air Force. As can be imagined, it caused considerable dismay and alarm in all quarters. Meanwhile, the Cabinet Mission requested the Viceroy for an appreciation of the situation that was likely to arise if their proposals fail and for a general policy on India in that event. In a Top Secret Memorandum dated 30 May

1946, Wavell made some interesting observations. The Congress, he felt, was determined to grasp all the power they can as quickly as possible. *"It is as if a starving prisoner was suddenly offered unlimited quantities of food ... his instinct is to seize it all at once ... also to eat as much and as quickly as possible, an action which is bound to have ill effects on his health."* As for Mahatma Gandhi, he was *"a pure political opportunist, and an extremely skilful one, whose guiding principle is to get rid of the hated British influence out of India as soon as possible."*

Wavell warned that if the Congress and Muslim League failed to come to terms, serious communal riots may break out, with very little warning, especially in the Punjab and the 'Mutiny Provinces' of UP and Bihar. Prompt action would be required to deal with the trouble, with very little time for consultations with London. He suggested that their actions should be based on certain definite principles, the first being to give India self-government as quickly as possible without disorder and chaos breaking out. It was important that Britain should avoid a situation in which she had to withdraw from India under circumstance of ignominy after widespread riots and attacks on Europeans, or adopt a course that could be treated as a policy of 'scuttle' or gave the appearance of weakness. While deciding the short-term policy, the long-term strategic interests of Britain should be safeguarded. In the event of serious trouble, there was a military plan, which provided for holding on to the principal ports—Calcutta, Madras, Bombay, Karachi—and to Delhi. Subsequently, British troops would be transferred from Southern India to the North. Stressing the need to avoid at all cost being embroiled with both Hindus and Muslims, he suggested a 'worst case' solution—to hand over the Hindu Provinces to the Congress and withdraw to the Muslim Provinces the North-West and North-East.[11]

Three days later, the Cabinet Mission and the Viceroy sent a 'Most Immediate' telegram to the Prime Minister, stressing the urgent need for the British Government to announce a clear policy in the event of the negotiations between the Cabinet Mission and the political parties breaking down. They expected the crisis to be reached any time between 5 and 15 June and the necessity for urgent decision on the line of action that the Viceroy was to adopt. The first point to be decided was whether they should attempt to repress a mass movement sponsored by the Congress and maintain the existing form of government. This was possible only if the Indian Army remained loyal, which was doubtful. It would also cause much bloodshed and achieve nothing, unless it was intended to stay on in India for another 10 to 20 years. At the other extreme was the decision to withdraw from the whole of India as soon as the Congress gave a call for a mass uprising. This would have an adverse impact on British prestige throughout the Commonwealth. After considering several options, the Cabinet Mission opined that if negotiations did in fact break down and they were faced with serious internal disorders, the situation would have to be met by adopting one of five courses. These were (1) complete withdrawal from India as soon as possible; (2) withdrawal by a certain date; (3) an appeal to the United Nations Organisation; (4) maintaining overall control throughout India; and (5) giving independence to Southern and Central India, and maintaining the existing position in North-West and North-East India.

The Plan recommended by the Cabinet Mission and the Viceroy was based on the last option, namely, *"to allow the six provinces of Madras, Bombay, Central Provinces and Berar, United Provinces, Bihar and Orissa, which are almost entirely Hindu, to become self-governing in every respect; but to maintain, for the time being the existing constitution in the remainder of British India, and the existing relationship with certain of the States. This would mean in effect giving independence to Southern and Central India and maintaining the existing position in North-West and North-East India."*[12]

The appreciations of the Viceroy and the Cabinet Mission reached London while the latter were still carrying out their negotiations in Delhi and Simla. They were considered by the Defence Committee of the Cabinet, which asked the Chiefs of Staff to examine the military implications of the five courses of action listed by the Cabinet Mission, keeping in mind the short-term policy and the long-term strategic interests listed by the Viceroy. The Report of the Chiefs of Staff, which was prepared without consulting General Headquarters India due to the short time available, figures in the Defence Committee Paper D.O. (46) 68 dated 12 June 1946, titled "INDIA-MILITARY IMPLICATIONS OF PROPOSED COURSES OF ACTION—REPORT BY THE CHIEFS OF STAFF". It is a remarkable document, which reveals the difference in the mindsets of 'imperialists' in London and the 'liberals' in Delhi. It also casts doubts on the intentions of the British Government, regarding granting independence to India.

Right at the beginning, the Chiefs of Staff—Alanbrooke, Cunningham and Tedder—spelt out the strategic requirements of Britain in India in any future war. It was emphasised that Britain should have recourse to India's industrial and manpower potential, and should be able to use her territory for operational and administrative bases, and air staging posts. It was therefore important that India should be secure from external aggression and internal disorder. For defence purposes, it was essential that she should remain a single unit. These were surprising assertions, considering that even at that moment, the Cabinet Mission was in Delhi, discussing with Indian leaders the form of self-governance that was to be introduced. It was also inconsistent with the Viceroy's stated views about giving India self-government as quickly as possible.

Before proceeding to examine the military implications of the courses proposed by the Cabinet Mission, the Chiefs of Staff eliminated the first three. The first and second courses that envisaged a complete withdrawal, with or without a time limit, were ruled out since they did not safeguard Britain's strategic interests. The third course of appealing to the United Nations had the disadvantage of freezing military action while the case was being debated, and was therefore unacceptable. That left only two courses, namely, maintaining control throughout India and a withdrawal in phases, which they proceeded to examine. The most important factor in retaining hold over the whole country was the ability to maintain law and order, which depended largely on the loyalty of the Indian armed forces. The conclusions on this crucial aspect were in line with those of General Headquarters India.

... We consider that the reliability of the Indian Army as a whole, including those in garrisons outside India is open to serious doubt. This applies even to Gurkha units ... The Royal Indian Navy and the Royal Indian Air Force cannot be regarded as reliable.

An important part of the Report deals with the reinforcements required to deal with internal disorders, based on estimates given by the Commander-in-Chief, India. In case the Indian Armed Forces remained loyal, it was estimated that in addition to the existing British forces then in India, reinforcements of three brigade groups and five air transport squadrons would be required. In the event of Indian troops becoming disaffected, the existing British forces and reinforcements mentioned earlier would be employed to hold key areas. To restore the situation in case of widespread disorder, additional reinforcements required would be between four and five British divisions, for which considerable administrative backing would also be needed. The Indian formations serving overseas would also have to be replaced by British formations. The requirement of reinforcements outside India was visualised as six brigades in Burma and Malaya; two brigades in Hong Kong and Japan; two battalions in the Dodecanese and three battalions in Iraq. The total British reinforcements thus came to five divisions for India; six brigades for Burma and Malaya and three battalions for Iraq.

The Report examined the availability of reinforcements and implications of providing them. There was at that time one British division in the Middle East; two in Greece; one in Italy and one division and seven brigades in Germany. Apart from the fact that pulling them out from these theatres would have serious security implications, it would need at least four months to move all the troops, equipment and vehicles to India, and that too at the expense of merchant shipping and vessels then engaged in carrying personnel home under demobilisation and repatriation programmes. The implications of maintaining the existing units in India up to their present strength would make it necessary to stop release in the formations concerned. In the interest of equality of treatment, it may become necessary to suspend release throughout the army and the other services. These would have a serious effect on morale as well as political repercussions.

The last course proposed by the Cabinet Mission was granting independence to Hindustan and withdrawing to Pakistan, comprising North-Western and North-Eastern India. This had several political and military implications, the most important being the division of India, which would preclude the establishment of a central authority to deal with defence, and in turn prejudice the future security of India against external attack. The armed forces would have to be reorganised and while India would have a strong army immediately, it would take many years for Pakistan to form an effective army of her own, making her susceptible to raids from the tribes on the North-West Frontier. There would be communal riots in the Punjab due to the large Hindu population in the area under British control in Pakistan. In Hindustan, the Muslims may be ill-treated. In the worst case, there may even be civil war, leading to British troops being involved in fighting with Hindustan and controlling communal strife in parts of Pakistan which have Hindu minorities. The Report concluded that withdrawal into Pakistan would not safeguard British strategic interests, could lead to civil wars and in the event that Congress opposed it, even lead to war. Hence, this option was completely unacceptable on military grounds.

The Report ended with the conclusions, which stated:

> ... A policy of remaining in India and firmly accepting responsibility for law and order would result, if the Indian Army remained loyal, in an acceptable military commitment and would safeguard our long term strategic interests. ... If however, the Indian Armed Forces did not remain loyal ... we would be faced with the necessity of providing five British divisions for India, with the consequent abandonment of commitments in other areas hitherto regarded as inescapable, serious effects on our import and export programmes and world-wide repercussions on the release scheme. The only alternative to this would be ignominious withdrawal from the hole of India.[13]

The Report by the Chiefs of Staff is an important document that brings to light several important points connected with India's independence. It clearly brings out the fact that the British Government was seriously considering the option of creating Pakistan in June 1946, not because of the lack of agreement with the political parties—this was still being negotiated by the Cabinet Mission—but due to the threat of disaffection in the Indian armed forces. This option was ruled out only because it did not serve British strategic interests. The disparity in the outlook of British officials in London and Delhi is also clearly visible; for the former, Britain's long-term strategic interest dictated continuation of British rule, while those closer to the scene of action, such as Wavell and Auchinleck, realised that it was time to go. Had the Indian armed forces remained loyal or had there been enough British divisions to keep them in check, the British would not have left India so soon.

Early in September 1946 the Viceroy forwarded to London a plan for phased withdrawal from India, which was a revised version of the Breakdown Plan of the Cabinet Mission. This was rejected by the British Government as it did not help British strategic interests. Wavell could see that the situation was steadily deteriorating, and unless a clear policy was announced, India could slide into anarchy. After consulting the Governors and the Commander-in-Chief, he estimated that the British could hold on for not more than 18 months. The Secretary of State, Lord Pethick-Lawrence, did not agree with Wavell's appreciation. He felt that it was still possible to hold on to India, and proposed further European recruitment to augment British troops in India. By this time, serious communal riots had broken out in East Bengal and in the Punjab, resulting in sizeable casualties among Hindus as well as Muslims. A new Interim Government headed by Jawaharlal Nehru had been installed at Delhi, with Sardar Baldev Singh as the defence member. In a letter dated 12 September to Auchinleck, who had recently been appointed a Field Marshal, Nehru discussed the withdrawal of British forces from India; pulling out Indian troops from the Netherlands, East Indies and Iraq; and the future of the Indian Army. In a broadcast to the Armed Forces on 9 October 1946, Baldev Singh announced the setting up of a committee to accelerate the pace of nationalisation. In view of these developments, Pethick-Lawrence's proposal to raise additional European troops for India appeared surreal.

Refusing to take no for an answer, Wavell sent a strongly worded note to the Secretary of State on 23 October in which he reiterated his demand for a firm declaration of the policy of the British Government. His plan, he wrote, was based on two main assumptions: (1) the object was to transfer power to India without undue delay and with the minimum of disorder and bloodshed; to secure the interests of the Minorities and to provide for the safety of the 90,000 Europeans in India; (2) the power of the British Government in India was weakening daily, and could not be sustained beyond 18 months. Using exceptionally strong language, Wavell made it clear that as the man on the spot, it was his responsibility to advise the Government of the action to be taken to achieve these objects. *"If the H.M.G. consider that my advice shows lack of balance and judgment, or that I have lost my nerve, it is of course their duty to inform me of this and to replace me"*, he wrote. *"But they take a very grave responsibility upon themselves if they simply neglect my advice."* Wavell ended by emphasising that they *"must have an emergency plan in readiness; and if it is agreed that we cannot hope to control events for longer than 18 months from now, we shall have to make up our minds and make a definite pronouncement at least in the first half of 1947. While I agree that we should not leave India till we have exhausted every possible means of securing a constitutional settlement, we can make no contribution to a settlement once we have lost all power of control."*[14]

In December 1946, the British Government invited Nehru, Baldev Singh, Jinnah and Liaquat Ali Khan to London for discussions, along with the Viceroy. During his visit, Wavell again pressed for adoption of the Breakdown Plan, urging the Government to announce that they would withdraw all control from India by March 1948. Some Cabinet Ministers such as Bevin and Alexander, who were imperialists at heart, balked at the prospect of a stark announcement of the ending of the British Raj. Prime Minister Attlee also felt strongly that the British should not relinquish control until at least a constitutional settlement had been reached. Since the chances of reaching an amicable settlement appeared dismal, Attlee's views seemed illusory. After a series of meetings the India and Burma Committee decided to recommend that 31 March 1948 should be announced as the date by which the British would hand over power in India. Wavell pressed for a firm announcement in this regard by the British Government. Attlee replied to Wavell on 21 December 1946, giving the impression that his proposal had been by and large accepted. Three days earlier, Attlee had offered Mountbatten the post of Viceroy in replacement of Wavell.[15]

Mountbatten reached India on 22 March 1947. Before he left London, he had been told that India would be granted independence by June 1948, that is, after 15 months; this was exactly what Wavell had been demanding for the last two years. On 23 May 1947, the British Cabinet approved, in principle, a draft Partition Plan, which was to be implemented in case of a failure to secure a final compromise. After consulting Indian political leaders, Mountbatten announced on 3 June 1947 that India would become independent on 15 August 1947. A few days later Mountbatten received the draft Indian Independence Bill, and was surprised to find that the British Government intended to retain the Andaman Islands, which were not to be regarded as a part of British India. It transpired that Britain was planning to make the Andamans a British Settlement. The recommendation to retain the islands had come from the British Chiefs of Staff, due to their strategic location in the Bay of Bengal, covering the sea routes to the East. Mountbatten strongly opposed the plan, informing London that any attempt *"to claim the Andaman Islands as colonies, to be treated in the same way as Aden, will cause an absolute flare-up throughout the length and breadth of India."* In view of Mountbatten's strong opposition, the British Government decided to drop the proposal.[16]

The crucial role of the Indian Armed Forces, especially the Indian Army, in the British decision to quit India has been commented on by several writers and historians. Captain Shahid Hamid, who was the Private Secretary to General Auchinleck, made the following entry in his diary on 30 March 1946:[17]

Today the Hindustan Times commented editorially on the Auk's appeal to the Indian Army. "There is no doubt whatever that if the transfer of power is not quickly brought about, the foreign rulers of India cannot count upon the loyalty of the Indian Army…"

The well-known historian, Dr. Tara Chand, has written:[18]

The most controversial measure of the Viceroy was the decision to advance the date of transfer of power from June 1948 to August 15, 1947. On this issue Mountbatten recorded his reasons in his conclusions appended to the Report on the Last Viceroyalty submitted to His Majesty's Government in September 1948. His defence for expediting the transference of power to the Indians was on these lines … "Secondly, the ultimate sanction of law and order, namely, the Army, presented difficulties for use as an instrument of government for maintenance of peace…"

Mangat Rai, a colleague of Penderel Moon in the Indian Civil Service before Independence, wrote an appreciation of the latter's book, *The British Conquest and Dominion of India*. Commenting on the role of the Indian Army he writes:[19]

How far were the competence and size of the Indian army factors in persuading the British to contemplate withdrawal from India, and in the final decision? In general Moon has consistent praise both for the sepoy regiments of the Company and for the Indian army's contribution in two world wars. He notes that at the end of the Second World War the army comprised two and a half million, in place of the 190,000 at the start. The army's record was brilliant marred only by the defection of comparatively small numbers to the Japanese-promoted INA. With an army of Indians of this calibre and size, would it have been practical to continue to govern India under British control?

Charles Raikes, a British Civil servant of the Mutiny days, had bluntly asserted that the British *"should legislate and govern India as the superior race"*, adding with some prescience, *"whenever that superiority ceases, our right to remain in India terminates also"*. This was in line with the view held by most Britons, who felt that British rule was a blessing for India. By the time World War II ended, the USA had assumed the mantle of the leader of the developed World, and her democratic principles of equality began to be embraced by other nations in the West. From the mutiny onwards, Indians had steadily acquired knowledge and skills that they had previously lacked, closing the gap between them and the British. According to Sir Penderel Moon:

> One noteworthy, but not often mentioned, example of change was the ending of the superiority of British to Indian troops, which had been a factor in the Company's original conquest of India. By 1943 Indian Divisions, in the opinion of Field Marshal Sir William Slim, were among the best in the world and divisional commanders on the Burma front called for Indian rather than British battalions. Thus Charles Raikes, if he had still been alive, would probably have felt obliged to admit that on his own premises the time had come for British withdrawal.[20]

The role of the Indian Army in the decision of the British to grant independence to India in 1947 is clearly established by the documents cited above, such as the letter written by the Viceroy, Lord Wavell to King George VI on 22 March 1946; the report by Sir J.A. Thorne, the Home Member of the Viceroy's Executive Council on the reliability of the Armed Forces submitted on 5 April 1946; the Note prepared by the Director of Intelligence, Brigadier B.P.T. O'Brien on the reliability of the three services on 15 April 1946; the report of the Cabinet delegation led by Sir Stafford Cripps and the Viceroy, Lord Wavell submitted to the Prime Minister, Mr. Attlee on 3 June 1946; the deliberations of the Defence Committee comprising the Chiefs of Staff on the military implications of the withdrawal plan proposed by the Cabinet Mission dated 12 June 1946;

the statements by the C-in-C in India, Field Marshal Claude Auchinleck during the meeting of the Chiefs of Staff in London on 13 August 1946; the Note by the C-in-C in India, the military aspects of the withdrawal plan submitted on 5 September 1946; the letter written by the Viceroy, Lord Wavell to Lord Pethick-Lawrence, the Secretary of State on 23 October 1946 advising a quick announcement of the date of transfer of power. In the last document the Viceroy has categorically stated that Britain will lose all power of control in India within 18 months.

All the documents mentioned above cite the unreliability of the Indian Army as the primary reason for the British withdrawal from India. The INA is not mentioned in any correspondence or deliberation of that period. The claim of some INA veterans in having played a major part in achieving independence from British rule is thus without basis. According to those who support this view, the mutinies in the RIN, RIAF and Indian Army that occurred in February 1946 were inspired by the INA. Since these mutinies were an indication that the Armed Forces could not be relied upon as an instrument of control, they triggered the decision of the British to quit India. Hence, indirectly, the INA was responsible for the decision to grant independence to India. This premise is flawed.

As explained in the chapters dealing with the mutinies, the underlying causes of the mutinies in the RIN and RIF were mostly administrative in nature. This included factors such as the low quality of food and lodging arrangements; differences in pay and rations compared to British troops; ill-treatment by superior officers; delay in demobilisation, etc. The political demands such as the release of the three INA personnel being tried in the Red Fort were added only after these were given wide publicity by the newspapers. In case of the Signals mutiny at Jubbulpore, the demands were differences in pay between IORs & BORS and poor quality of rations. There were two questions to which answers were demanded. Why was fire opened on RIN ratings? Why were two INA officers sentenced to seven years RI when others were merely cashiered?

The trial of Shah Nawaz Khan, Gurubaksh Singh Dhillon and Prem Sahgal was held between November and December 1945 in the Red Fort.

They were tried for "waging war against the King Emperor" in a public court martial. Before this several trials of INA prisoners had been held at various places in the country. A large number of leaders of various political parties formed a defence committee to defend the three accused. This was given wide publicity and they began to be called freedom fighters. Though they were initially held guilty and given various terms of punishment, these were later commuted by the C-in-C in view of the widespread protest. It is relevant that the three mutinies occurred in February 1946, almost three months after the Red Fort trials. If they were inspired by the INA trials, why did the mutineers wait for three months?

Subsequently another INA officer, Captain Burhanuddin, was tried by a military court. Brig K. M. Cariappa was the presiding officer of the court. The charges against Burhanuddin were for atrocities committed against other INA soldiers, resulting in the death of Teja Singh during his interrogation and torture. He was found guilty, and Cariappa announced the sentence of 7 years rigorous imprisonment. Surprisingly, there was no protest or publicity of this trial, as there had been in the Red Fort trials a few months earlier. In his letter addressed to King George VI on 22 March 1946, the Viceroy, Lord Wavell wrote:

> The I.N.A. trials have sunk to a back page of the Press now that they reveal the brutalities inflicted on the loyal prisoners. These are the trials which should have taken place first. It was undoubtedly a serious blunder to place on trial first men against whom no brutality could be proved. Congress turned on the best legal brains in India to defend them, and the full force of a completely unscrupulous and irresponsible propaganda by the Press and in political speeches, to exalt these men into national heroes. Having obtained their effect, they now almost ignore the brutalities revealed in later trials.[21]

Apart from holding the trials of Shah Nawaz Khan, Gurubaksh Singh Dhillon and Prem Sahgal first, before the trial of others such as Burhanuddin who were charged with heinous crimes, as mentioned by the Viceroy, the other mistake committed by the British authorities was to hold the trials in public, at the Red Fort. Field Marshal Auckinleck, the C-in-C, also regretted his decision to hold the trials in public, which gave unnecessary publicity to the accused. This was seized on by the political parties to organise protests against British rule. Surprisingly, none of the political leaders who joined the INA defence committee to defend the accused at the Red Fort trials came forward to defend Burhanuddin.

Almost all documents pertaining to the period 1946-1947 assert that it was the reliability of the Indian Army, rather than the other two services, that caused the most concern to the British authorities in India. In a Note on the Military Aspects of the Plan dated 5 September 1946, the C-in-C Field Marshal Auchinleck wrote:[22]

1. The importance of keeping the Indian Army steady is emphasised. It is the one disciplined force in which communal interests are subordinated to duty, and on it depends the stability of the country.
2. The steadiness of the RIN and the RIAF is of lesser import but any general disaffection in them is likely seriously to affect the reliability of the Army.

Mutinies in the Army are not uncommon. In the Indian Army, there were several mutinies before and after the Great Indian Mutiny of 1857, when almost the whole of the Bengal Army revolted, almost ending British rule in India. Thereafter there was only one major mutiny up to the outbreak of World War II. This was the mutiny in Singapore in 1915, involving the Muslims of the 5th Light Infantry. There was also a relatively minor uprising in the 2/18 Royal Garhwal Rifles in 1930 at Peshawar. During World War II there were a number of mutinies, all of them involving Sikh troops. After the end of World War II, the only major mutiny that had occurred in the Indian Army was the one in the Signals Training Centre at Jubbulpore in February 1946.

There are several documents that cast doubts on the reliability of the Indian Army after World War II, in which it had covered itself with glory.

In some detailed assessments, it has been clearly mentioned that in the Army, the Signal Corps cannot be depended upon to control protests against British rule that were increasing day by day. The decision to grant independence as well as the advancement of the date from June 1948 to August 1947 were the result of these assessments. Had the mutiny in the Signals Training Centre at Jubbulpore not taken place in February 1946, it is doubtful if the British would have withdrawn so suddenly. Of course, independence was likely to come soon, but it may have been delayed by 5-10 years.

It is interesting to reflect on the course of history if the Indian soldier had not been affected by nationalistic feelings and continued to serve loyally as he had during and before World War II. Though the freedom movement had developed considerable momentum by the time the war ended, the assumption that it would have achieved independence on its own would be erroneous. With the vast resources at their disposal, it would not have been difficult for the British authorities in India to muzzle the movement, as they had done in 1930 and 1942. The only reason for them not being able to resort to such measures after 1945 was the uncertain dependability of the Army, especially the Corps of Signals. Had the Indian soldier remained staunch, or adequate British forces been available, it is most unlikely that freedom would have come in 1947. If nothing else, it would have been delayed by 10-15 years. If this had happened, perhaps India would not have been partitioned, the Kashmir problem would not have existed, and the Indo-Pak wars of 1948, 1965 and 1971 would not have been fought. Who knows, with its large size, population and a long spell of peace unfettered by the threat of war, India would have been a World power, equalling or even surpassing China by the turn of the century.

Notes
1. Sir Penderel Moon, *The British Conquest and Dominion of India*, London, Duckworth, 1989), p. 1092, quoting S. Gopal, *Jawaharlal Nehru* (1975-79), vol. 1, p. 263.
2. Lt Gen S.L. Menezes, *Fidelity & Honour - The Indian Army from the Seventeenth to the Twenty First Century*, Penguin, (New Delhi, 1993), p. 345.
3. Penderel Moon, *The British Conquest and Dominion of India*, London, Duckworth,

1989, p. 1109.
4. Moon, p. 1122.
5. Moon, pp. 1136-1138.
6. Moon, p. 1140.
7. Maj Gen D.K. Palit, *Major General A.A. Rudra—His Service in Three Armies and Two World Wars*, Reliance Publishing House, (New Delhi, 1997), p. 277.
8. Nicholas Mansergh and Penderel Moon (eds.), *The Transfer of Power 1942-47* (12 vols., London), vi, pp. 1233-1237.
9. Mansergh and Moon, *The Transfer of Power*, vii, p. 150.
10. Mansergh and Moon, *The Transfer of Power*, vii, pp. 406-407.
11. Mansergh and Moon, *The Transfer of Power*, vii, pp. 731-737.
12. Mansergh and Moon, *The Transfer of Power*, vii, pp. 787-795.
13. Mansergh and Moon, *The Transfer of Power*, vii, pp. 889-900.
14. Mansergh and Moon, *The Transfer of Power*, viii, pp.794-799.
15. Moon, pp. 1164-1165.
16. Mansergh and Moon, *The Transfer of Power*, xi, p. 306.
17. Major General Shahid Hamid, *Disastrous Twilight* (London, 1986), p. 47.
18. Dr. Tara Chand, *History of the Freedom Movement in India*, Publications Division, Ministry of Information and Broadcasting (1967).
19. Moon, pp. 1195.
20. Moon, p. 1187.
21. Mansergh and Moon, *The Transfer of Power*, vi, pp.1232-1235; Wavell papers; Private Correspondence: H.M. The King, pp. 110-114.
22. Mansergh and Moon, *The Transfer of Power*, viii, p. 462.

Bibliography

Primary Sources

'Report of Commission of Inquiry – The RIN Mutiny 1946', Document No. 601/7968/1, History Division, Ministry of Defence, New Delhi.

'A Brief History of Events Associated with the Disaffection and Strikes among personnel in RAF Units of Air Command, SE Asia', Document No. 601/9768/4, History Division, Ministry of Defence, New Delhi.

Correspondence Files, Signals Training Centre, 1946, Corps of Signals Museum, Jabalpur.

Secondary Sources

Barreto, Brig. T., *History of the Corps of Signals, Volume 1*, New Delhi, 1975.

Bose, Sugata, *His Majesty's Opponent: Subhas Chandra Bose and India's Struggle against Empire*, Harvard University Press, 2011.

Cardozo, Maj. Gen. Ian (ed.), *The Indian Army - A Brief History*, New Delhi, United Service Institution of India, 2005.

Chand, Dr Tara, *History of the Freedom Movement in India*, New Delhi, Publications Division, Ministry of Information and Broadcasting, 1967.

Cohen, Stephen, *The Indian Army: Its Contribution to the Development of a Nation*, Delhi, Oxford University Press, 1990.

Connell, John, *Auchinleck – A Critical Biography*, Cassel & Compnay, 1959.

Corr, Gerard H., *The War of the Springing Tigers*, London, Osprey Publishing House, 1975.

Das, Dilip Kumar, *Revisiting Talwar – A Study in the Royal Indian Navy Uprising of February 1946*, New Delhi, 1993.

Dasgupta, Jayant *Japanese in Andaman & Nicobar Islands. Red Sun over Black Water;* Delhi, Manas Publications, 2002.

Deedes, Lt Gen. Sir Ralph B., *Historical Records of the Royal Garhwal Rifles, Vol II, 1923-1947*, New Delhi, 1962.

Dutt, B.C, *Mutiny of the Innocents,* Bombay, Sindhu Publications, 1971.

Evans, Humphrey, *Thimayya of India*, Dehradun, Natraj Publishers, 1988.

Fay, Peter Ward, *The Forgotten Army*, University of Michigan Press, 1993.

Forrest, G.W., *A History of the Indian Mutiny*, London, Blackwood, 1904.

Mahatma Gandhi, *Collected Works, Vol. 1 to 98*, Wardha, Gandhi Sevagram Ashram.

Gordon, Leonard A. *Brothers against the Raj: a biography of Indian nationalists Sarat and Subhas Chandra Bose*, Columbia University Press, 1990.

Hamid, Maj Gen Shahid, *Disastrous Twilight*, London, 1986.

James, L., *Mutiny in the British and Commonwealth Forces 1757-1956*, London, Buchan and Enright, 1987.

Kasliwal, R.M., *The Impact of Netaji and INA on India's Independence*, UBS Publisher's Distributors, 2005.

Khan, Maj Gen Shah Nawaz, *My Memories of INA & its Netaji*, Delhi, Rajkamal Publications, 1946.
Lebra, Joyce C., *Jungle Alliance—Japan and the Indian National Army*, Asia Pacific Press, Singapore, 1971.
Mansergh N. and Penderel Moon, (ed.) *The Transfer of Power, Vols VI to VIII*, HMSO, London.
Mason, Philip, *A Matter of Honour*, London, 1974.
————— *The Men Who Ruled India*, New York, 1985.
Mathur, L.P., *Kala Pani. History of the Andaman & Nicobar Islands with a study of India's Freedom Struggle*, Delhi, Eastern Book Corporation, 1985.
Menezes, Lt. Gen. S.L., *Fidelity and Honour – The Indian Army from the Seventeenth to the Twenty First Century*, New Delhi, Penguin, 1993.
Mohan Singh, Maj. Gen., *Soldiers' Contribution to Indian Independence*, Army Educational Stores, New Delhi, 1974.
Moon, Penderel, *The British Conquest and Dominion of India*, London, Duckworth, 1989.
Palit, Maj Gen D.K., *Major General A.A Rudra – His Service in Three Armies and Two World Wars*, New Delhi, Reliance Publishing House, 1997.
Pelinka, Anton, *Democracy Indian Style –Subhas Chandra Bose and the Creation of India's Political Culture*, Routeledge, 2003.
Perry, F.W., *The Commonwealth Armies – Manpower and Reorganization in Two World Wars*, Manchester University Press, 1988.
Prasad, Bisheshwar (ed.), *Official History of the Indian Armed Forces in the Second World War 1939-45 – India and the War*, History Division, Ministry of Defence, New Delhi, 1966.
Praval, K.C., *Indian Army After Independence*, New Delhi, Lancer Publishers, 2009.
Saigal, Air Cmde A.L. (ed.), *Birth of An Air Force – The Memoirs of Air Vice Marshal Harjinder Singh*, New Delhi, 1977.
Sareen, T.R., *Secret Documents of the Singapore Mutiny*, Delhi, Mounto Publishers, 1995.
———, *Japan and the Indian National Army*, Agam Prakashan, 1986.
———, *Indian National Army – A Documentary Study*, New Delhi, Gyan Publishing House, 2004.
Singh, Lt Gen Harbaksh, *In the Line of Duty – A Soldier Remembers*, New Delhi, Lancer, 2000.
Singh, Rear Admiral Satyindra, *Under Two Ensigns – The Indian Navy 1945-1950*, New Delhi, 1986.
Singh, Maj. Gen. V.K., *Leadership in the Indian Army – Biographies of Twelve Soldiers*, New Delhi, Sage, 2005.
———, *History of the Corps of Signals, Volume II*, New Delhi, 2006.
———, *Contribution of the Armed Forces to the Freedom Movement in India*, New Delhi, 2009.
Sivaram, M., *The Road to Delhi*, Institute of Southeast Asian Studies, 2012.
Thomas, Lt. Gen. Mathew, and Jasjit Mansingh, *Lt. Gen. P.S. Bhagat, PVSM, VC*, New Delhi, Lancer, 1994.
Thorat, Lt. Gen. S.P.P., *From Reveille to Retreat*, New Delhi, Allied Publishers, 1986.
Toye, Hugh, *The Springing Tiger*, London, Cassell Publishers, 1959.

Wavell, *The Viceroy's Journal,* London, Oxford University Press, 1973.
Yadav, S.S., *Forgotten Warriors of Indian War of Independence 1941-1946* (Indian National Army), Gurgaon, 2005.

www.ingramcontent.com/pod-product-compliance
Lightning Source LLC
Chambersburg PA
CBHW020122010526
44115CB00008B/931